ECONOMIC AND SOCIAL COMMISSION
FOR ASIA AND THE PACIFIC

STUDIES ON WOMEN IN DEVELOPMENT | 2 |

PROMOTING WOMEN'S RIGHTS
AS HUMAN RIGHTS

UNITED NATIONS

New York, 1999

ST/ESCAP/1974

UNITED NATIONS PUBLICATION
Sales No. E.00.II.F.53
Copyright © United Nations 1999
ISBN: 92-1-120003-2

FOREWORD

The adoption of a human rights framework to improve the status of women in the public and private spheres has led to some progress in the last two decades in the promotion of the equality of women and men. However, women and men still face differences in the realization of their human rights. These differences are often the result of prevailing cultural and social values and of legal traditions which maintain discriminatory practices, thereby diluting the hard-fought gains made.

The Fourth World Conference on Women, held at Beijing in 1995, reaffirmed that women's rights are human rights. It provided the momentum needed to focus global attention on achieving the objectives of the Nairobi Forward-looking Strategies for the Advancement of Women before the year 2000.

The Expert Group Meeting on Promoting Women's Rights as Human Rights was organized by ESCAP in collaboration with the National Women's Education Centre of Japan. It was held at Saitama, Japan from 7 to 9 August 1996. The Meeting brought together experts from the Asian and Pacific region to review critically the progress made in the ESCAP region towards women's equality with men in the field of human rights. The discussions led to the completion of an ESCAP study, *Human Rights and the Legal Status of Women in the Asian and Pacific Region,* which was published as the first in a series entitled Studies on Women in Development.

The present publication has three parts. Part one presents the report of the Expert Group Meeting. Part two contains the general statement of the Expert Group, their recommendations and the follow-up actions proposed to realize the recommendations. Part three contains the background country papers presented by the participants at the Meeting.

It is hoped that this publication will be disseminated widely to enable women in Asia and the Pacific to discuss the commonality of the problems faced by them and to share positive developments and experiences in order to strengthen their efforts to achieve human rights and the equal legal status of women in civil and private life.

Adrianus Mooy
Executive Secretary

CONTENTS

CONTENTS *(continued)*

PART ONE

Report of the Expert Group Meeting on Promoting Women's Rights as Human Rights

INTRODUCTION

Women's rights have traditionally been viewed as separate from human rights. Yet, throughout their lifetime, women are often faced with violations of their human rights, with such violations often taking the form of gender-based violence and discrimination. The Jakarta Declaration for the Advancement of Women in Asia and the Pacific and the related plan of action, which were adopted in June 1994 by the Second Asian and Pacific Ministerial Conference on Women in Development, and the Beijing Platform for Action adopted in September 1995 by the Fourth World Conference on Women, identified the protection and promotion of the human rights of women as an issue of critical concern.

The United Nations has played an important role in setting international standards for recognizing the human rights of women. One of the most noteworthy outcomes of its efforts is the Convention on the Elimination of All Forms of Discrimination against Women (CEDAW), which was adopted by the General Assembly in 1979. More than 150 States have acceded to or ratified the Convention. Another watershed for women's rights is the Vienna Declaration and Programme of Action, adopted in 1993 by the World Conference on Human Rights, which called for the elimination of violence against women in public and private life. In the same year, the United Nations also adopted the Declaration on the Elimination of Violence against Women and it appointed a Special Rapporteur on Violence against Women.

To follow up these developments, ESCAP, in collaboration with the National Women's Education Centre (NWEC) of Japan, organized the Expert Group Meeting on Promoting Women's Rights as Human Rights. The Meeting, which was held at Saitama, Japan, from 7 to 9 August 1996, was challenged to answer the question, "How do women have legal rights in their lives and what are the obstacles towards exercising these rights?". To do so, it reviewed the progress achieved in the ESCAP region in treating women's rights as human rights, and it formulated recommendations on women's legal rights and the elimination of violence against women.

I. ORGANIZATION OF THE MEETING

A. Attendance

The Meeting was attended by 11 experts, among whom were lawyers and directors of organizations working on issues relating to women's human rights in the Asian and Pacific region. Three resource persons and representatives of United Nations Bodies also attended the Meeting.

B. Opening Statements

The representative of the ESCAP Secretariat, the Chief of the Women in Development Section of the Rural and Urban Development Division, delivered the opening statement. She stressed that the current Meeting was especially significant because it was one of the first activities to follow up the implementation of the Beijing Platform for Action, in which women's rights were recognized as women's rights. She pointed out that women still suffered from gender-based discrimination and violence. The United Nations, however, was making efforts to protect and promote women's rights as human rights, and governments had been responding positively to those efforts.

Noting that violence against women was one of the topics that would be discussed at the Meeting, the ESCAP representative referred to the extent of that problem in the region. A positive development in recent years was the increased involvement of non-governmental organizations (NGOs) and civil society in the fight against violence. She stressed that the important task of the current Meeting was to identify strategies to address key concerns relating to women's rights as human rights. She was confident that the collective knowledge and experience of the experts would result in recommendations that would help women in the region in their struggle for development and human rights.

Following the statement of the ESCAP representative, an opening statement was delivered by Ms Teruko Ohno, Director General, National Women's Education Centre (NWEC). After welcoming all participants, Ms Ohno spoke about establishment of NWEC, which was created in 1977 by the Ministry of Education, Science, Sports and Culture, for the promotion of non-formal education for adult women. It was the only governmental women's centre in Japan. Since 1977 NWEC had accommodated close to two million visitors. Ms Ohno then proceeded to introduce the initiatives which NWEC had been taking in Japan to follow up on the Fourth World Conference on Women. Most notably, those activities had included the Centre's role as the national focal point on information related to women, as part of efforts to promote and strengthen women's information Centre through the Women's Information Network System (WINET) which had connected over 300 institutes, including women's centres and universities in Japan.

C. Agenda

The following agenda was adopted by the Meeting.

1. Opening of the Meeting.

2. Regional overview on women's rights as human rights:

    (a) Status of women's legal rights, including application of international human rights standards;

    (b) Situation of violence against women.

3. Women's legal rights; problems and possible measures to improve their legal status:

    (a) Nationality law;

    (b) Family law: working towards universal standards;

    (c) Basic needs as basic rights: inheritance, property and employment laws;

    (d) Reproductive rights.

4. Violence against women; situation and possible measures to eliminate violence against women:

    (a) Domestic violence, including wife beating, wife abuse and marital rape, dowry murders, infanticides, foeticide, incest, forced sterilization and abortion;

    (b) Sexual exploitation and prostitution;

    (c) Violence against refugee and internally displaced women.

5. Formulation of recommendations.

6. Adoption of report.

II. REGIONAL OVERVIEW

The Meeting covered two theme topics; women's legal rights and the elimination of violence against women. First, Dr Savitri Goonesekere, ESCAP consultant and resource person, made a presentation on the regional overview of women's rights as human rights. She presented the historical development of the women's rights issues from the perspective of international law and human rights jurisprudence, and highlighted how the involvement of women's groups in various United Nations conferences had brought the issue of women's rights as human rights to the surface and had opened up the debate on human rights which had eventually provoked the need to internalize these human rights standards at the national level. It was pressure from women's groups in particular that had led to the wide ratification of the United Nations Convention on the Elimination of All Forms of Discrimination against Women. The Beijing Platform for Action later made a clear linkage between women's rights and human rights. The realization of women's rights, she emphasized, must be perceived as an agenda that recognized the right of women to reach their maximum potential as human beings on the basis of entitlement rather than as beneficiaries of welfare policies.

She then focused on some specific problems in the Asian and Pacific region with regard to the internationalization of the human rights ideology as the vital framework of national laws and policies. Some countries in the Asian and Pacific region had a positive record in the realization of basic needs as basic rights. This experience needed to be shared, without being used as a rationale that denied the importance of realizing equality through the protection of other human rights such as personal liberty, political rights and freedom of information and expression. The region's contribution to human rights would promote recognition of the reality that NGOs, civil society and communitarian values had an important role in realizing the interests of the people at the national and international levels. The concept of human rights could help to forge a new social contract which was not purely individualistic and exclusively rights oriented, a social contract between citizens as individuals and as members of communities, and their governments. The rights and duty-based relationship between them arose from a combination of civic responsibility and accountable governance.

At the end of her presentation, she suggested ways to integrate human rights standards within countries. Various constitutional developments within countries of the region had helped to integrate human rights standards. The concept of basic needs as basic rights could be forged in countries, particularly in South Asia which had not provided access to basic services so as to compel governments to allocate resources. The concept of "state action" had been used to develop accountability of officials for inaction in law enforcement. The manner in which *locus standi* to bring cases before the courts had been widened to enable NGOs and activists to address the courts on infringements when individuals lacked the capacity to enforce their rights was an example of "State action". All those developments had helped women to obtain access to justice in order to challenge discrimination.

Strategies such as the preparation of alternative NGO reports to the CEDAW monitoring committee, and scrutinizing national reports and strengthening of national monitoring bodies appeared important for integrating human rights standards on gender equality at the national level. It was also crucial that women of Asia and the Pacific helped to expand the scope of current international standards to include their own experiences. As the commonality of problems faced by women and the relevance of a human rights approach in improving women's situation was reflected in the country experiences of the region, it was important to reflect, take stock, and develop positive experiences to work towards eliminating the infringement of human rights and the entrenched discrimination that could be seen across the Asian and Pacific region.

Following extensive discussions on each agenda item, the experts formulated recommendations on women's legal rights and violence against women. Those concerned the laws of nationality and domicile, family law, economic rights, reproductive rights, domestic violence and prostitution and trafficking in women and girls. The conclusions and recommendations are contained in part two of this report.

A general statement was also formulated by the experts during the meeting. The general statement is contained in part two of the present report.

Annex

LIST OF EXPERTS

Ms Shanti Dariam, Director, IWRAW (International Women's Rights Action Watch), Malaysia

Dr Savitri Goonesekere, Faculty of Law, University of Colombo, Sri Lanka

Ms Imrana Jalal, Resource Trainer, Pacific Regional Human Rights Education, Fiji

Ms Hina Jilani, Director, AGHS Law Associates, Pakistan

Dr Meera Kosambi, Director, Research Centre for Women's Studies, India

Ms Serey Phal Kien, President, Cambodian Women's Development Association, Cambodia

Ms Marfua Tokhtakhodzhaeva, Women's Resource Centre, Uzbekistan

Dr Salma Sobhan, Executive Director, ASK Human Rights and Legal Aid Centre, Bangladesh

Ms Aurora De Dios, Executive Director, Coalition Against Trafficking in Women in Asia and the Pacific, Philippines

Ms Sapana Pradhan Malla, Forum for Women, Law and Development, Nepal

Ms Ngo Ba Thanh, Vice President, Viet Nam Lawyers Association, Viet Nam

Ms Hiroko Hashimoto, Associate Professor, Jumonji University

PART TWO

Conclusions and Recommendations, Follow-up Action and General Statement of the Expert Group Meeting

I. CONCLUSIONS AND RECOMMENDATIONS

A. Laws on nationality and domicile

Most constitutions of the region which are the supreme law of the land grant equal rights to men and women and make discrimination on the grounds of sex unlawful. Despite this general principle of equality within some constitutions themselves, principles of citizenship discriminate against women. If the citizenship, residence or domicile laws within the constitution do not abrogate the basic principle of equal rights for women, other statutes or policies deprive women of full citizenship rights that are enjoyed by men. Such contradictions and anomalies are an infringement on women's right to equality.   Some glaring examples are as follows.

In some countries, if a woman marries a foreigner she automatically loses her citizenship in her country of origin as it is assumed that she will assume the citizenship and domicile of her foreign husband. If she does not lose her citizenship automatically she usually has to leave her country of citizenship anyway as her foreign husband has no right to apply for citizenship or residency. She thus loses the most important right of citizenship, her right to live in her country of citizenship.

Men can, in general, transfer their nationality to their foreign wives upon marriage. The foreign wives of men automatically have the right to reside or apply for citizenship rights by virtue of marriage. However the foreign husbands of women do not enjoy a similar right. Women thus have to leave their country of citizenship.

Children usually acquire citizenship rights through their fathers and not their mothers. This means that women cannot transfer their nationality to their children by descent. Where both father and mother are citizens and the child is born within the country the mother nevertheless cannot transfer citizenship. In some countries when children are born within their mother's country of citizenship then they have a right to be citizens of that country. In some countries if children are born outside their mother's country of citizenship they cannot become citizens of their mothers' country unless their father is also a citizen of that country. No similar restrictions on citizenship rights are placed on the children of men married to foreign women whether or not they are born within or outside their father's country of citizenship.

In some countries women acquire the domicile of their husbands and cannot apply for matrimonial orders unless they apply in the country where their husbands are domiciled. This has serious implications for women who are deserted or who have to leave the country of their husband's domicile and who require maintenance, divorce or custody orders regarding their children.

If women who have lost their citizenship upon marriage to a foreigner are divorced, separated or widowed in some countries they cannot re-acquire citizenship of their country of origin for themselves or their children.

Women who marry foreigners and move to their husband's country of citizenship often suffer when they leave their husbands due to violent abusive relationships because when they separate they have not become eligible for citizenship in their husband's country of citizenship.

All these laws are in breach of article 9 of CEDAW. All States party to CEDAW should be urged to comply with article 9. States which have reservations on article 9 should be urged to withdraw their reservations.

All States should be urged to ratify the Married Women's Nationality Convention (1962).

All legislation within the constitutions and in other statutes should be changed to give equal rights to men and women so that they may transfer their citizenship to their foreign spouse and to their children in all circumstances.

If a foreign spouse does not wish to acquire the citizenship of his or her spouse he or she should have rights of residency in his or her spouse's country of citizenship.

A person's domicile should be his or her domicile of choice regardless of where his or her spouse is domiciled.

B. Family law

The family, whether nuclear or joint, is seen as a unit of production, productivity and privacy. Its unity is therefore promoted and protected, often at the expense of individual members. We should broaden our definition of family to include other groupings of dependency and solidarity. In respect of the family as conceptualized by most of the family laws of the region, we should move away from conventional assumptions about who should be designated the head of family and also recognize the autonomy of each member.

1. Marriage

Consent of the bride must be a legal requirement. It must be given in the presence of a neutral authority. The minimal age for marriage must be the same for both parties. No consideration should be payable by either party (dowry/dower).

2. Divorce

Breakdown of marriage as evidenced by a minimum period of separation should be recognized as grounds for dissolution of the marriage by divorce. Matrimonial offenses relating to mental cruelty and physical violence and failure to maintain should also be grounds for divorce.

Provision should be made for non-molestation orders to be made against an abusive partner. Laws on divorce based on these principles are vital to ensure the human rights of women within marriage.

3. Matrimonial property

Any property acquired during the continuance of the relationship should be deemed jointly acquired and joint property. The wife/female partner should be entitled to remain in the home, where it is a single unit family. In a joint family, suitable (similar) accommodation must be found for the wife. Shelter homes or halfway homes must be available for such wife/ female partners. In the case of an abusive partner, he should not have information about the location, etc. An administrative unit would handle renting, etc.

4. Guardianship and custody

Both parents should be regarded as joint natural guardians of their child. In the event of separation/divorce "the best interests" of the child should be the determining factor.

5. Maintenance

During this period of unequal socio-economic status of women in relation to men, law should ensure adequate maintenance for divorced/separated wives.

6. Family courts

Family courts should be set up. There should be an expeditious disposal of cases. No family court procedures should infringe on a woman's human rights or her autonomy.

7. Adoption

Adopting in the sense of the adopted child becoming part of the adopting family should be recognized. Inheritance should devolve to such a child. Adopted children should have the same rights as natural children in all respects.

8. Non-marital children

The concept of illegitimacy should be removed from the legal system. The marital status of parents should have no bearing on the status of children born outside marriage and they should have equal rights.

Laws and policies on the illegitimacy of a child born outside marriage should be reviewed and reformed to reflect the gender equality mandates of CEDAW. The legal relationship of the child to the parents should be determined in accordance with the best interests of the child.

9. Head of family/children's name

A child should be identified as the child of both its parents and either parent's names should be sufficient to fulfil the requirement of identification of the child. A woman should have the legal right to carry her name even after marriage and to confer it on her children.

C. Economic rights

1. Basic needs as basic rights

In some countries of the region, girls and women do not have access to basic services in the areas of health, nutrition, safe water, sanitation, and education and therefore have diminished life chances, and no opportunities for economic advancement. Access to good quality services is vital to realize not merely economic rights but the related rights to survival, development and personal security. Allocation of resources for compulsory primary and secondary education and health, registration of birth and marriage, is crucial to ensure that women have maximum opportunities for education, training and productive economic activities that can improve their quality of life.

Provisions in national constitutions on directive principles of state policy should be integrated with the fundamental right to personal security and life so that socio-economic rights are perceived as an integrated dimension of the right to personal security and life, and gender equality. CEDAW standards that have been accepted by ratifying countries recognize that the provision of basic services is a dimension of the right of personal security and life, rather than a state effort to provide social welfare benefits.

2. Access to employment and economic advancement

Women should be provided with opportunities for economic advancement beyond survival, on the basis of equal partnership with men in the family and community. The concept of equal wages for comparable work and equal opportunities for promotion without gender-based discrimination should be recognized through legal action and administrative policies. Where necessary, affirmative action policies such as quotas in favour of women should be introduced as a temporary measure in line with article 4 of CEDAW. Such quota systems should be accompanied by policy initiatives on education and training for women to ensure that women are brought into the mainstream of economic activity and can compete with men on the basis of equal qualification and merit. Quota systems should also be introduced in sectors where qualified women are not emerging as holders of the highest executive or administrative positions.

Maternity leave legislation and facilities for the care of the elderly and disabled should be recognized in laws and administrative policy on the basis that these are not "benefits" to woman workers but rather a support system for caregivers. Efforts should be made to recognize the concept of leave for both men and women to fulfil family responsibilities as caregivers. Law and policy should move towards the recognition of "maternity leave" for the health of a pregnant women worker and "parental leave" for the realization of the survival and development rights of children under the Convention on the Rights of the Child and CEDAW.

Sexual harassment on the way to work and at the work place impacts adversely on a woman's working environment and her economic productivity, and prevents her enjoying equal rights in the employment sector. Laws and supporting policies should be introduced in all countries to address the problem of sexual harassment.

3. Strengthening family laws that impact on economic rights

Laws on inheritance rights, contractual capacity, distribution of property on divorce and in state land allocation schemes should conform with the CEDAW standard of providing equal access to economic advancement. Legal systems in all countries should recognize that women have the right to equal inheritance. However, where females receive fixed portions of family property in systems of personal law or according to religious norms, efforts should be made to develop legal concepts in national law that will ensure that females in the family obtain financial compensation or equal access to land and other assets.

4. Special areas of concern

The situation of women in the informal sector, including the agricultural sector, requires regulation to protect women's rights as workers. Social security schemes should be developed by the state for self-employed women and all women workers.

Occupational health standards in the formal sector, particularly in free trade zones and home-based production connected to industry must be put in place. States should take steps to ratify and implement ILO standards on home-based workers.

Women migrant workers are generally vulnerable to violence including sexual exploitation and trafficking as well as oppressive working conditions. Often their status as illegal immigrants impacts adversely on their lives and their families. States should provide programmes for adequate health and social services and respect the human rights of migrant workers.

In countries with transitional economies, the concept of "land use right" as distinct from land ownership should be developed to ensure that women have the equal right to transfer, mortgage, lease/rent or occupy land, houses and other economic assets.

Since men are in fact often the heads of households, conferring separate rights for land use is not sufficient. Consequently, women should have the right to have their names entered as joint holders of land in certificates that confer land use rights. Such certificates should give access to secondary benefits, such as credit and various other services connected with use of land. Women should qualify for tax exemption for some time.

Owing to the collapse of the former system of state subsidies, in the transition period, women have no choice but to work hard for low pay, without health benefits, maternity leave or access to child care, health services and schooling facilities for children. New social security arrangements should be developed to provide an adequate support system to enable women to combine work and family responsibilities, on the basis that fulfillment of basic needs such as health and education are basic socio-economic rights.

Women should have the right to be both beneficiaries of and contributors to the new market economy on the basis of full equality with men. Although the constitution and the law recognize the equal right to engage in economic activity and business, women's right to engage in business is in fact denied because they have no access to capital, new technology or training. Efforts should be made to provide training in entrepreneurship and small business management for women and to give them access to credit facilities.

D. Reproductive rights

It is necessary to recognize that women/couples have the right to determine family size, and that contraceptives, therefore, need to be made easily available.

It is necessary to recognize the constraints to family planning:

- Family planning methods are often geared to population control policies rather than to women's health or the couple's choice. Therefore, coercion is often involved.

- Acceptability of contraceptives often depends on religious or other beliefs.

- Even when abortion is legal and easily available, there can be a danger of sex-selective abortion due to a strong son preference.

- This strong son preference often creates an unwillingness to limit family size.

Legal provisions relating to working women are necessary, for example, maternity leave and related provisions.

Sexuality and reproduction are usually closely linked to the institution of marriage. This means that there is a stigma attached to illegitimate children which has repercussions for the incidence of maternal mortality. The fact of adolescent sexuality and contraceptive requirements also need to be recognized.

Maternal health needs to be adequately cared for through recognition of women's right of access to good quality services for reproductive health. Lack of access to contraceptives and good health services often has fatal consequences for women, such as infanticide, child abandonment, septic abortion and maternal death.

A women's right to make a voluntary and informed choice on the use of contraceptives must be recognized and respected.

E. Domestic violence

1. Need for conceptual clarity

In all countries of the region, there are customary and traditional practices which continue to foster and legitimize the use of domestic violence against women. Laws should be developed in conformity with international standards in a concerted effort to eliminate these practices.

Domestic violence refers to violence that is perpetrated against women members of the family in the home because they are women. There is a misconception that all women are safe in the home. Violence is not an aberration of an individual who has at that moment in time lost control. It is a manifestation of socially condoned hierarchical gender relationship and a form of control over women.

In order to distinguish between the dynamics of gender-based violence and other forms of violence, it is recommended that the term "domestic violence" be replaced by the term "criminal assault against women in the family".

Women are inhibited from seeking redress for this violation because of accusations that they are contributing to the breakup of the family. This has serious and long-term implications as it contributes to the malfunctioning of the family and curtails the enjoyment of all other rights of women. Domestic violence is a grave obstacle to the achievement of equality between women and men.

It may occur in the private sphere but it is not a private matter. It is a violation of the fundamental right to personal security and bodily integrity and diminishes the personhood of women. It may not be justified on any grounds such as the grounds of provocation, or that of culture or tradition. Domestic violence is a crime and the state has a responsibility to provide adequate mechanisms for both short-term and long-term measures to combat it.

State inaction in responding to domestic violence needs to be seen as an infringement of women's human rights.

2. Education and training

Many myths still prevail at all levels, within the community and the agencies of the state (police, judiciary, etc.), which justify domestic violence.

Equality between women and men is still not an appreciated value. Education to bring about attitudinal changes, and to instil respect for women's rights and for the principle of equality between women and men needs to be integrated into school curricula.

The skills for efficient and gender sensitive investigation and prosecution are inadequate. Gender sensitization is essential for the police, prosecutors and the judiciary. Women are unaware of their rights. Conscientization, mobilization and rights awareness education for women are critical.

3. Mechanisms for redress

The response of the legal system in most instances is inadequate. Substantive and procedural laws have not facilitated the application of human rights standards in the treatment of this crime. Where the laws have been adequate, their enforcement has been weak for a variety of reasons including that of inadequate policy resources or lack of access for women to legal aid. The courts have sometimes trivialized the issue.

It is not enough to strengthen penal provisions. Gender bias in other legal provisions for ancillary claims, guardianship/custody and domicile prohibit women from taking action.

Women in custody are at times further abused by the police. Specific legal provisions should be introduced and combined with administrative instruction with regard to discipline in law enforcement.

4. Linkages and networking

Effective measures for addressing the problem require inter-agency collaboration such as through hospitals, the police, welfare, and legal agencies. It also requires GO/NGO collaboration. All of this does not exist in a systematic manner. Responses of this nature have been ad hoc.

5. Resistance from the community and family

Women who break away from abusive relationships are ostracized and often exposed to other forms of risk. Activists face a risk too.

Programmes attempting to deal with domestic violence need to take cognizance of this risk and be proactive in this regard.

6. Support services

There is a need for support services in the interim if holistic responses are to be given.

These services need to comprise temporary shelters, counselling, information, legal support, medical assistance and a host of other services essential for enabling women to either break out of abusive relationships or to be reconciled according to their choice.

The policy of shelters must keep in mind that women's human rights cannot be violated in the name of protection. Illegal custodial control over women should not be used under any circumstances.

Social policy for housing for female heads of households, skills training for adult women and special schemes for creating employment opportunities for women who have been out of the labour market for some time need to be advocated.

7. NGO activism

NGO activism is often reactive and ad hoc.

Such activism has to be evaluated and NGOs need to engage in activism that is holistic, proactive and sustained.

NGO efforts to assist victims of domestic violence should be supported with adequate resource allocations from governments.

F. Prostitution and trafficking in women and girls

Trafficking of women for purposes of prostitution has become an issue without borders, affecting countries within Asia as well as other parts of the world such as North America, Europe and the Middle East. The numbers of women and girls victimized by this criminal activity is staggering. Trafficking of women today is highly syndicated, and even globalized and technologized.

The trafficking flow has been from Asia to Europe, North America and the Middle East and since the collapse of the Soviet bloc, trafficking has also been occurring from Eastern Europe to Asia, Europe and parts of North America.

Equally significant has been the rise of trafficking incidents from some Asian countries to Asian high growth economies. Asia has thus become the locus of trafficking of women, as the source of trafficked women and the destination of men involved in sex tourism.

Trafficking for purposes of prostitution and sexual exploitation has various forms such as the following:

- Cross-border trafficking characterized by abduction and kidnapping of women and girls;

- Trafficking via migration channels enticing women as domestic helpers or entertainers through recruitment agencies, tourist agencies and impresarios;

- Trafficking for the purpose of marriage where recruitment is done via marriage matching agencies, pen-pal clubs, Internet, advertisements, etc. Under certain circumstances, trafficking of women has also occurred in places where there are shortages of women of marriageable age. Fake marriages are sometimes contracted as a way to recruit women for prostitution or as unpaid labourers or domestic helpers;

- There is trafficking for high-end prostitution in clubs, discos, casinos and resorts catering to rich clients, and trafficking for low-end prostitution to serve plantation workers, dock workers and others.

Trafficking in women for prostitution has deep-rooted causes arising from the unequal gender relations of men and women and the structural disparities and inequalities of power and resources between developed and developing countries and between slow growing economies and high growth economies.

While poverty of women and their families is often a powerful driving force for women to enter prostitution or to be vulnerable to the enticements of traffickers, the mainstreaming of consumerist culture, including that of prostitution, has created the climate for the acceptance of prostitution as an economic option for many impoverished families.

Trafficking for prostitution purposes exists locally but it has increased significantly due to foreign demand by both Asian and Western men for the sexual services of women and increasingly for young girls. The global crisis in HIV/AIDS has generated a big demand for young girls who are perceived to be free of HIV/AIDS infection because they are virgins.

Government policies that stress income generation through tourism and export of female labour have sometimes resulted in the creation of opportunities for the facilitation of trafficking. The fact that governments also derive revenues from tourism and labour export makes governments even more accountable to the problem of trafficking.

The impact of trafficking on women and young girls has been devastating. Kidnapping, abductions, rape and other form of sexual violence, beatings and torture, illegal confinement and detention, denial of identity papers and sexual harassment are some features of this trade. Male concepts of sex that is paid often give them a licence to inflict sadistic acts of violence on prostitutes.

Women trafficked for purposes of prostitution are exposed to constant threats to their personal safety at every stage of the trafficking process at the hands of traffickers, law enforcement personnel, and male buyers of sex.

An increasing number of women have become afflicted with HIV/AIDS and other sexually transmitted diseases (STDs) as a result of which they become even more vulnerable to abuse and neglect. Their human rights are often violated and many have been forcefully repatriated, but upon return to their families, they are also rejected and ostracized.

Women in prostitution often cannot even invoke their human rights as they are stigmatized in all societies and are perceived to have no rights whatsoever. Society's valuing of virginity has also caused trafficked women to devalue themselves even more.

The core issues in trafficking for prostitution are the dehumanization of women as sex objects and their alienation from their body and bodily integrity as well as their exposure to high levels of violence. Thus the human rights that should be asserted by victims of trafficking for prostitution is the human right not to be prostituted and to be free from violence. In addition they should have rights to personal safety and to a decent and humane source of livelihood.

1. National strategies

In view of the human costs of trafficking and the devastating impact of HIV/AIDS on women and young girls, states should give highest priority to addressing this urgent problem.

Adequate laws to address local and international trafficking of women should be enacted. These laws should not criminalize the women but should strengthen sanctions against traffickers.

Monitoring, investigation, and research programmes on trafficking of women, particularly on the demand side of prostitution should be initiated and strengthened.

Intervention/action programmes should be developed in the following areas;

(i) Preventive actions including education/awareness raising, family support services, community development, shelters for women and girls who run away from home as well as advocacy for police and legislative reforms;

(ii) Emergency response including rescue police action operations, counselling and therapy for victims and families, family tracing programmes, medical aid, shelters for women and girls escaping from prostitution, and legal assistance;

(iii)   Rehabilitation of victims and those involved in prostitution should include education programmes, social, economic and employment generation programmes, shelters, long-term arrangements for housing, skills training, community awareness and other support systems;

(iv)   Upgrading of knowledge, skills, capability and gender sensitivity of law enforcement agencies in preventive, emergency and rehabilitation work;

(v)   Strengthening of coordination mechanisms among law enforcement agencies, NGOs and communities for effective implementation of anti-trafficking programmes.

Special programmes to assist HIV/AID victims should be implemented immediately.

2. Regional strategies

Regional bodies such as the Association of Southeast Asian Nations (ASEAN) and the South Asian Association for Regional Cooperation (SAARC) should decisively address the problem of cross-border trafficking, sex tourism and other forms of trafficking at the highest policy level.   These should include coordinated police monitoring and investigation of trafficking syndicates.

Bilateral agreements should be explored to address this critical problem in the spirit of states parties' obligations under CEDAW and the Convention on the Rights of the Child.

Temporary residence permits should be considered in cases of trafficked women and girls.   Repatriation of victims should not be done forcibly and in cases of voluntary repatriation, the home country should ensure the availability of social, health and economic support services.

Safe humane and decent treatment of trafficked women should be provided while in custody.

Gender sensitivity training of law enforcement personnel dealing with trafficking victims should be provided.   A policewomen force should be trained to handle trafficking of women cases.

Laws should address the issue of male demand for prostitution.

Development of an accurate regional database on trafficking and a regional emergency and assistance system and procedure should be developed.

3. International strategies

The 1949 Convention for the Suppression of the Traffic in Persons and of the Exploitation of the Prostitution of Others should be reviewed to take into account the specific dimensions of prostitution and trafficking in the Asian and Pacific region and to consider the possibility of a new convention.

Countries should consider the issue of extraterritoriality to penalize male nationals who commit trafficking for the prostitution of women and children.

Temporary residence permits should be granted to women who had been trafficked and for women who have been trapped in violent arranged marriages.

Social services such as health, shelters and economic assistance programmes should be provided by the receiving countries.

G. Refugee women

The climate of conflict in some countries in the region has created serious problems affecting the situation of internally displaced women, refugee women, and internally displaced women in need of international protection. The gender dimension of their problems and their special vulnerability to infringement of their human rights have often not received attention. The complex nature of their problems and the difficult issues they raise must be examined carefully in order to formulate special initiatives at the national, regional and international level.

Refugee women, other displaced women in need of international protection and internally displaced women are extremely vulnerable and under higher risk due to the following:

- Restriction of mobility
- Non-application of laws of the host country
- Lack of access to courts
- Lack of social support system available in the settled environment
- Frequent incidence of violence against them by refugee camp administrators, other refugees, including other male family members
- High incidence of trafficking in and sales of refugee women, other displaced women in need of international protection and internally displaced women.

Measures and steps, in line with UNHCR Sexual Violence against Refugees Guidelines on Prevention and Response; Geneva Convention on Protection of Civilian Persons in Time of War and Declaration of the Human Rights of Individuals Who are not Nationals of the Country in which They Live (1985) article 5.1(a), should be taken to protect the safety and physical integrity of refugee women, other displaced women in need of international protection and internally displaced women from violence and sexual assault against them by refugee camp administrators and other refugees.

Measures should be taken to prevent the trafficking in and sale of refugee women, other displaced women in need of international protection and internally displaced women for the purpose of slave labour and prostitution.

Adequate social support services like health, counselling, and education, should be provided to refugee women, other displaced women in need of international protection and internally displaced women.

II. FOLLOW-UP ACTION

Further to the above conclusions and recommendations, the following suggestions were made for possible future projects:

- Sharing responses to domestic violence and coming up with best practices to protect and promote women's rights as human rights;

- Producing a video on trafficking along the lines of the WHO video "Why did Ms X die?";

- Assessing the impact of CEDAW on policy changes as CEDAW has regular reporting requirements and redress procedures;

- Disseminating, popularizing, and promoting acceptability of CEDAW;

- Commissioning a case book/material that will provide information on country experience on the interaction of integrating a standard on equality into national law/policy in the areas of (i) contractual capacity and inheritance; and (ii) maternity and parental leave, and social security;

- Developing a directory of research institutions working in the areas of economic rights and women's issues, with a view to building a database and establishing a monitoring network on country performance on the economic rights of women. An expert group meeting can be called for this purpose and entrusted with the initial task of developing targets of achievement for a specified period and monitoring indicators. The group can also work towards preparing an annual report on the economic status of women, for selected countries in the Asian and Pacific region. These reports could be widely circulated and published so that they: (i) can be used in advocacy to demonstrate the comparative performance of countries; and (ii) will provide useful information in preparing country and alternative NGO reports to CEDAW.

III. GENERAL STATEMENT OF THE
EXPERT GROUP MEETING

Two third of the States Parties in the ESCAP region have ratified CEDAW as of March 1996. By ratifying CEDAW, they have taken an important first step in committing themselves to work towards realizing a common standard of gender equality and the universal interdependent, interrelated human rights of women under international law.

They have reaffirmed the following core principles:

1. No issue of national sovereignty, cultural specificity or religious precept can constitute a constraint to the achievement of women's human rights.

2. Standards of gender equality cannot be realized except by recognizing the basic socio-economic rights of women. The lack of access to economic opportunities and basic services prevents women from exercising their human rights.

3. Advancement of the status of women is closely related to social and economic rights which can only be realized by making adequate resources available. Women's right to equal access to opportunities for social and economic advancement should be recognized.

    Some emerging economic policies may have the potential for creating new economic opportunities for women. However, trade liberalization and free market policies, and structural adjustment programmes initiated without sensitivity to women's concerns are threatening to undermine the advancement of women. Women's right to participate in the formulation of these crucial policies has become vital. Women's participation is necessary to ensure that economic policies are formulated in such a way that they do not prejudice the realization of gender equality and the advancement of women.

    High allocation of national resources to defense expenditure has taken crucial resources away from social sector development, making it difficult to fulfil the commitments of states under CEDAW. Militarization of states has created a climate of conflict and undermined the potential for regional and international cooperation and peace. This environment of conflict has exposed women to extreme forms of violence and caused the breakdown of civil institutions.

4. Violence against women is an infringement of a woman's right to personal security and prevents the enjoyment of all other rights guaranteed by CEDAW.

    The standards of CEDAW should be developed and applied by reference to general recommendation No. 19 of CEDAW on violence against women and the United Nations Declaration on the Elimination of Violence against Women so as to respond to problems of violence against women including trafficking and sexual exploitation which have emerged as critical concerns in the region.

By ratifying CEDAW, states have accepted the commitment to establish institutional mechanisms for monitoring the situation of women and to take action to implement the full range of obligations under international law. However, existing mechanisms at the national level have not been found to be effective and adequate. They need to be strengthened with the full participation of government and NGOs.

Infringement of women's human rights can occur in any country. Absence of a complaints procedure for individuals and organizations at the international level has prevented cases of infringement of women's human rights receiving publicity and has denied remedies to victims who have failed to obtain redress within their own countries. Therefore, all States parties to CEDAW are urged to endorse the Optimal Protocol that is now under consideration by the Commission on the Status of Women.

Women's human rights cannot be realized in a vacuum. For the best implementation of CEDAW, it is necessary to strengthen linkages to other international human rights instruments including the Convention on the Rights of the Child. Efforts should be made to promote and foster networking between national agencies and organizations working on human rights.

PART THREE

Country Papers

I. REGIONAL OVERVIEW*

The concept that women's rights is an intrinsic dimension of human rights is considered a comparatively recent development. There was a time when the human rights jurisprudence that had developed in international law was considered irrelevant to women's experience. However within the last decade, women's groups have discovered the importance of taking ownership of human rights jurisprudence and using it as a strategy for realizing gender equality.

The involvement of women's groups in the United Nations conferences in Vienna, Cairo and Copenhagen led to the clear articulation of statements that recognized the need to view issues of importance to women from a rights perspective. It is pressure from women's groups in particular that led to the wide ratification of the United Nations Convention on the Elimination of All Forms of Discrimination against Women (CEDAW, 1979). Although the Forward-looking Strategies developed at the World Conference on Women to Review and Appraise the Achievements of the United Nations Decade for Women: Equality, Development and Peace, held in Nairobi in 1985 referred to the objective of obtaining wide ratification of this Convention, there had been very little progress in this regard within the decade. The momentum for wide ratification grew in the post-Vienna period. By the time the Fourth World Conference on Women was held in Beijing in 1995, many more countries had been persuaded to ratify the Convention. The Beijing Platform for Action has made a clear linkage between women's rights and human rights. The realization of women's rights must therefore be perceived as an agenda that recognizes the right of women to reach their maximum potential as human beings on the basis of entitlement rather than as beneficiaries of welfare policies.

International human rights standards have been enshrined in the Universal Declaration of Human Rights (1948) and the two International Covenants on Civil and Political Rights and Economic, Social and Cultural Rights (1966). CEDAW and Convention on the Rights of the Child (CRC, 1989) which articulate a clear concept of gender equality, recognize that women's rights require the realization of both civil and political rights as well as access to basic needs such as health, nutrition, education and shelter. The connection of women's rights to human rights and the Asian critique of the over-focus on civil and political rights has contributed to a jurisprudential development in international law which recognizes that both sets of rights are interdependent and integrated. The linkage established to human rights has also led to a growing recognition that priority should be given to addressing issues of gender discrimination in partnership with men, at the national level. It is necessary that linkages are forged with other human rights treaty bodies such as the Human Rights Committee of the International Covenant on Civil and Political Rights. These bodies as well as the monitoring committee of CEDAW and CEDAW must be used to realize an agenda of gender equality.

---

* Summary of an ESCAP study entitled *Human Rights and Legal Status of Women in the Asian and Pacific Region* by Savitri Goonesekere, Professor of Law, Sri Lanka, published by ESCAP in the Studies on Women in Development series.

The linkages made between human rights and women's rights have also contributed to the development that views gender-based violence against women as an infringement of their human right to bodily integrity, personal liberty and security. The trivialization of violence against women has been almost global. The United Nations Declaration on the Elimination of Violence against Women (1993) was a major step in addressing the issue of violence against women as a human rights infringement.

Despite these positive developments, there have been some specific problems in the Asia and Pacific region in regard to the internationalization of the human rights ideology as the vital framework of national laws and policies. In particular, human rights are sometimes considered Eurocentric rather than universal. This paper presents the view that human rights are about the abuse of power and that women in the Asian and Pacific region need to take ownership of human rights, using them to obtain government accountability at the national level.

The paper argues that in this region, the centre of government must hold, with governmental policy continuing to be an important strategy for realizing gender equality. The disintegration of the centre through internal strife worsens the position of women. The experience of South Asia shows that government intervention is necessary to realize gender equality, and that human rights jurisprudence can be used to contain abuse and obtain accountability in governance. Cultural relativist approaches are dangerous because they contribute to reinforcing gender discrimination that has acquired legitimacy through the historical experience of most societies over centuries. A universal agenda on human rights can be forged by giving priority to core concerns such as the realization of socio-economic rights and the elimination and prevention of violence against women. It has been suggested that the realization of these core norms provides a basis for developing common norms applicable to all women in this region, despite differences of ethnicity, religion and nationality.

Some countries in the Asian and Pacific region have a positive record in the realization of basic needs as basic rights. This experience needs to be shared, without being used as a rationale that denies the importance of realizing equality through the protection of other human rights, such as personal liberty, political rights and freedom of information and expression. This region's contribution to human rights can promote recognition of the reality that NGOs, civil society and communitarian values have an important role in realizing the interests of the people at the national and international levels. International human rights instruments endorse the rights of "the people". Human rights standards need to be realized within countries as the rights attendant on citizenship. The concept of human rights can help to forge a new social contract which is not purely individualistic and exclusively rights oriented, a social contract between citizens as individuals and as members of communities, and their governments. The rights and duty-based relationship between them arises from a combination of civic responsibility and accountable governance.

Human rights standards can be integrated within countries in many ways. National constitutions provide a powerful mechanism for internalizing these standards.

This paper discusses the various constitutional developments within countries of the region that have helped to integrate human rights standards. It refers in particular to developments in South Asia that have interpreted a right to life as a right to basic needs. The concept of "state action" has been used to develop accountability of officials for inaction in law enforcement. The paper refers to the manner in which *locus standi* (the right to litigate) to bring cases before the courts has been widened to enable NGOs and activists to address the courts on infringements when individuals lack the capacity to enforce their rights. All these developments help women to obtain access to justice in order to challenge discrimination.

Constitutional strategies such as the imposition of quotas for women are discussed in the paper as affirmative action to redress the historical injustices that women have faced. A new model of equality based on disadvantages rather than differences seems to be emerging. The paper addresses the issue of conflict between cultural relativism and human rights standards in the experiences of the Asian and Pacific countries where plural legal systems apply differently to women on the basis of ethnicity and religion. There have been positive as well as negative experiences in working towards human rights standards. There appears to be a general consensus on the urgent need to realize a common model of equality based on the human rights standards of CEDAW, and move beyond elimination of differences. Reservations entered by countries to CEDAW need to be constantly scrutinized and reviewed so that they are not an obstacle to realizing a common agenda for all women.

Country experiences suggest that discriminatory laws and policies can be found in the areas of family law, nationality, economic rights and violence against women even in countries where Constitutions reflect the human rights norm of gender equality. The problems of women's reproductive health and violence against women represent new challenges for legal systems and policy planning, since laws and policies have not perceived these problems as involving human rights issues. There is an urgent need to share positive experiences in all these areas and to move towards a common perspective on the problems affecting women which are similar across the region.

The ratification of CEDAW has provided a basis for cooperation between governments and NGOs in monitoring the realization of human rights commitments. National bodies appear to be weak and the absence of an individual complaints procedure that will give women and women's groups access to international bodies is felt to be a definite need. Strategies such as the preparation of alternative NGOs reports to the CEDAW monitoring committee, and scrutinizing national reports and strengthening of national monitoring bodies appear important for integrating human rights standards on gender equality at the national level. It is also crucial that women of Asia and the Pacific help to expand the scope of current international standards to include their own experiences. The 1949 United Nations Convention for the Suppression of the Traffic in Persons and of the Exploitation of the Prostitution of Others is an example of a major international treaty that does not reflect the anguished experience of Asian women and girls constantly exposed to a contemporary form of slavery through forced prostitution and cross-border trafficking.

The experience of the region in the last decade suggests that there are many visible failures in working towards an effective human rights agenda to realize substantive rather than formal equality for women. Nevertheless, there have also been invisible successes. An agenda of human rights requires a complex strategy of law and policy, allocation of national resources and the awareness and vigilance of women as well as men of good will. The commonality of problems faced by women and the relevance of a human rights approach in improving women's situation is reflected in the country experiences of the region. If we are to work towards eliminating the infringement of human rights and the entrenched discrimination that is seen across the Asian and Pacific region, it is important to reflect, take stock, and develop positive experiences.

II. BANGLADESH*

A. Introduction

Bangladesh came into existence in 1971 separating from the state of Pakistan which had been formed in 1947 when India was partitioned following the withdrawal from the subcontinent of the British colonial rulers. Bangladesh the eastern wing of Pakistan was known as East Pakistan. In undivided India Bangladesh formed the eastern part of the state of Bengal. West Bengal remains a part of India.

Bangladesh is a fertile delta plain of about 55,000 square miles. It has a large population, about 120 million, and an agrarian economy. About 85 per cent of the population is rural based.

The population of Bangladesh is a young one with nearly 47 per cent of its population under the age of 15 years. Males historically have outnumbered females though occasionally a reverse ratio is found at certain ages. The majority of the citizens of Bangladesh are Muslim. About 10 per cent are Hindu and the tribal population of around 10 million is largely Buddhist. There are a few hundred thousand Christians.

The Child Marriage Restraint Act 1929 – amended over the years – and the Dowry Prohibition Act 1983, were enacted to control the social evils of child marriage and the giving of dowry to the groom in consideration of marriage. Yet there are inherent gaps in these laws. The rise of dowry is a direct result of wide age differences in marriage. A wide age gap in marriage means that at any given time there are many more eligible women around than there are men. This adverse ratio gets worse in fast growing populations. This advantage to men contributes to the high incidence of a demand for dowry. Though not the only reason for the rise in dowry demands, there is certainly a correlation between the age of marriage for a girl and the demand for a dowry. At present the minimum ages of marriage is 18 years for a girl and 21 for a man.

A democratic system of government in Bangladesh was finally achieved in 1991 after several years of popular unrest which culminated in the overthrow of President Ershad. While it would be too soon to say that agitational politics and confrontation have given way to democratic processes, a (diminishing) band of optimists feel that a window of opportunity has opened. Women are mustering strength to prevail upon the Government to implement its international commitments. In 1984 the Government of Bangladesh ratified the Convention on the Elimination of All forms of Discrimination Against Women (CEDAW) with reservations to articles 2, 13 (a) and 16 1 (c) and (f). Their stated reasons were that these articles

---

* By Dr Salma Sobhan, Executive Director, ASK Human Rights and Legal Aid Centre, Bangladesh.

were in conflict with the Shariah law. This was no more than a subjective pronouncement. The Women's Movement in Bangladesh is pressing the Government to withdraw these reservations which derogate from the Constitution of Bangladesh.

Under the Constitution of Bangladesh there is guarantee of equal rights to men and women. This fundamental right is, however, not only eroded by social and customary practices and attitudes as happens almost everywhere in the world but the article guaranteeing freedom of conscience is in practice used to qualify the scope of the article on equality. While it is argued that the bulk of the law governing Bangladesh is gender-neutral this is not, in fact, so. It is true that, the laws of personal status aside, they are not, by and large, overtly discriminatory. Nonetheless there is an undoubted patriarchal coloration to the whole legal system and much that is given with the one hand is taken away by the other.

B. The women's movement

Since the 1950s, women of the then East (and West) Pakistan, now Bangladesh, have been demanding an equitable share in decision-making processes as well as just laws for themselves. The Muslim Family Law Ordinance 1961 was a positive outcome of such struggles.

The Dowry Prohibition Act (1990), Cruelty to Women (Deterrent Punishment) Ordinance, 1983, (now repealed) Women and Children Repression Act, 1995 and the Family Court Ordinance of 1985 were all achieved basically because women of Bangladesh continued to pressure the government. None of these Acts, however, is satisfactory. One of the negative aspects of these Acts is that they give more power to the police and less to the courts. The Family Court Ordinance retains the adversarial system and the same courts are used except that, on designated days, family matters will be listed. Nonetheless despite these and other shortcomings these Acts do represent steps forward for the women's movement.

C. Women and the law

The laws at present governing Bangladesh were, for the most part, introduced by the British in the nineteenth century. These were derived from the English Common Law and are codified. A notable exception is the laws of personal status, i.e. laws governing marriage, divorce, maintenance, guardianship and custody of children and inheritance, which are an amalgam of customary practices derived from religious sources. Different communities are governed by the religious laws and customary practices of their putative faiths. Some of these laws have also been codified. Legal principles have also been extended and developed by judicial pronouncements.

The Constitution of Bangladesh passed in 1972 enshrined the principles of secularism and social justice for which the people had been campaigning since 1952. Successive authoritarian governments have, however, eroded these. The principle of secularism was removed. Islam was made the state religion and the ban on religious parties from participating in politics was lifted. Over the years the state has become more autocratic and sectarian.

1. Nationality

Rights to citizenship are discriminatory being conferred at birth through the paternal line, and at marriage through the husband.

Under the Laws of Bangladesh citizenship may be acquired by birth, descent, marriage, migration or naturalization. Each mode of acquisition other than through birth, is subject to criteria which discriminate against women.

The right to confer citizenship by marriage is only open to Bangladeshi males. A man in the service of the Government of Bangladesh will have to get a "No Objection Certificate" from his employer before marrying a foreigner. A woman would probably have to resign.

2. Family law

Equality in the marital sphere is limited by the failure to recognize the Constitutional principle of equality as applicable to the private sphere. The Muslim Family Law Ordinance 1961 regulates certain aspects of discrimination in these matters but its effects are more palliative than curative. In any case it is only applicable to Muslims. Though India in 1956 made sweeping changes in the laws applicable to Hindus, none of these changes are reflected in the Hindu Law applicable in Bangladesh. The Christians are in an even more parlous state as the laws governing them are a product of late Victorian attitudes and have hardly been modified since.

(a) Marriage

The bride's consent is a requirement in both Muslim and Christian law. A Hindu girl's consent is not a legal requirement as giving her in marriage is a duty imposed upon her father for his own salvation. Theoretically, an adult Muslim woman can even disown a marriage contracted on her behalf by her guardian when she was a minor. In practice, short of her standing up and shouting her refusal to the marriage, her consent is deemed to have been given willingly no matter how coercively obtained. A failure to obtain even a coerced consent would, however, be grounds for invalidating both Christian and Muslim marriages. Under the school of law governing most Muslims in the subcontinent (Hanafi) an adult Muslim woman does not need her guardian or wali's consent to her marriage. There is also case law from the Bombay High Court where Muslim women have been held as having the right to choose to be governed by the school of law of her choice.

None of the three main religious communities countenance interfaith marriage. The Christian Church may allow such a union if the non-Christian partner agrees to some conditions. There is no such authority within Islam. The question hardly arises for Hindu women where even inter-caste marriages are prohibited. The Special Marriages Act allows a form of civil marriage. It requires a statement from both contracting parties that neither professes any faith. This Act has been modified in India and this requirement has been removed there but not in Bangladesh.

(b) Dowry/dower

Under Muslim law, the pre-Islamic bride price was converted into a marriage settlement or dower called *meher*. In the Middle East and other parts of the Muslim world, this is paid to the bride at the time of marriage as it is regarded as an incident of marriage. In the subcontinent it is regarded as payable only on divorce or widowhood. In practice it remains unpaid more often than not. In the middle classes a high figure is often negotiated to act as a deterrent to the husband in the exercise of his right of repudiation.

In Victorian and earlier times in England an heiress might lose her entire fortune upon marriage unless it was tied up at the time the marriage took place (in what would today be called a prenuptial agreement). The later and more progressive Married Woman's Property Act 1937 would probably still be applicable to Christian couples today.

Hindu girls had, and in Bangladesh continue to have, very limited rights to paternal property. They received instead a dowry at the time of marriage as considerable as the family could afford to compensate them for this very limited right of inheritance. This was called *stridhan*. This *stridhan* or dowry is different from a demand for money made by the groom or his family at the time of marriage as consideration for the marriage which is a new social evil also referred to as dowry. An anti-dowry act has been passed to regulate and prohibit such demands. This Act has been strengthened from time to time to make such a demand a cognizable offence and to increase the penalties but has not really been very effectively implemented. *Meher* has been exempted from the application of the Dowry Prohibition Act but the Act is silent on *stridhan*. The Hindu bride is therefore in an even more invidious position than before.

(c) Divorce

Divorce is not recognized at all under Hindu Law. While marriage is a sacrament both under Hindu Law and the Canon Law, Christians can seek a civil dissolution of their marriage under the Christian Marriages and Divorce Act. A Hindu man can, however, if dissatisfied with his lot marry polygamously. A Hindu wife has no such option. She may, however, live separated from her husband particularly if he has married again. Though there is a High Court decision that a suit for the restitution of conjugal rights should now be barred on the grounds that it violates the Constitutional provisions of equality, in any case a decree, even if granted, would not be enforced.

A Hindu widow may now remarry but if she does she forfeits any interest she might have in her late husband's estate. This is so even if she belongs to a caste which before the passing of this Act recognized a woman's right to remarriage.

The Christian Marriages and Divorce Act allows a Christian husband to divorce his wife for the offence of adultery. She, however, needs to establish both the offence of adultery and another offence – desertion, cruelty or bestiality. Even an innocent wife can expect in the case of divorce no more than a settlement of one third of her husband's income. If the situation is reversed and the wife is a woman of means her husband may receive as much as two thirds of her fortune if she is the guilty party. While the concepts of matrimonial offence etc. are now being phased out elsewhere, they are valid for Christians in Bangladesh (and the subcontinent).

Under Muslim law a Muslim man has the right unilaterally to repudiate his wife at will. He may delegate her this right at the time of marriage or later but unless he does so, she has to seek dissolution of her marriage proving a matrimonial offence under the Muslim Marriages Dissolution Act (1939). She may also offer to forgo or return her dower in order that the Court may pass an order dissolving her marriage if she cannot allege a matrimonial offence but is seeking a dissolution (this is called *Khula*). Divorce by mutual consent is recognized, as well as many esoteric variants. However, the Muslim Family Law Ordinance lays down that however the divorce be pronounced, certain procedures must be followed for the divorce to be effective. A notice of divorce must be served on the wife and three months must elapse after receipt of such notice before the divorce becomes effective. Theoretically, the husband is bound to maintain his wife financially until the divorce becomes final. A declaration made by a deserting husband that he had divorced his wife by writing memos "months ago" to her would now not stand as an effective divorce. However, as there is a one-year limitation period on demanding prior maintenance, this right is not of much practical use to a wife. Further, the fact that divorces are frequently registered before they are final or before the wife has been given appropriate notice have resulted in all sorts of legal complications. By failing to register a divorce, a husband may also keep his wife in a state of limbo.

(d) Guardianship and custody

Christian and Hindu women are egregiously discriminated against here since in law the custody of even a nursing baby may be given to the father. While a Muslim mother is entitled to her young children's control (under Hanafi Law: sons until aged seven, daughters until puberty), she too is often, in practice, deprived of the custody of her young children. Though the Guardian and Wards Act lays down that a child's best interest is the criterion for deciding on guardianship and custody (the father is always the guardian of the child otherwise, whether Hindu, Muslim or Christian), quite often where a mother has been unjustifiedly denied her natural custody, over a period of time the status quo has been used as the guiding principle to determine the "best interest" of the child.

(e) Polygamy

Muslim and Hindu men may practise polygamy. Christian marriages are monogamous. Certain procedures introduced under the Muslim Family Law Ordinance 1961 make it theoretically less easy for a Muslim man to marry during the existence of a continuing marriage but even when improperly entered into, the marriages remain valid (as indeed do child marriages and underage marriages).

(f) Reproductive rights

A woman's control over her own body is imperfectly recognized. The fact that marital rape is not recognized is an indication of this. So are the constraints surrounding family planning; her husband's permission is required. (Unmarried women will find it difficult to get advice and help about contraception.) The anomaly here is that while a woman is not seen as having plenary control over her body, she is responsible for controlling her fertility. All the family planning programmes are geared towards the control of her fertility.

D. Women and economic rights

1. Inheritance

(a) Muslim women

The Islamic Law of inheritance or Quranic Laws came as a superstructure on the body of the law prevalent in tribal Arabia. Originally, the tribal laws allowed only male agnates to succeed to property. No woman, however, of any degree was an heir. Muslim laws made women as well as men competent to inherit. The list of what are usually called the Quranic heir, included 12 new heirs of whom eight are females. These are wife, mother, daughter, sister (full, consanguine and uterine), son's daughter and grandmother (obviously not all of them can inherit simultaneously: there are priorities within the list). Since the Koran is to be likened to an amending act rather an exhaustive code women were not given parity in the matter of their shares and as a general rule, the female is given one-half the share of the male. In the changed society of the present century, where there is little reason to perpetuate this distinction, however, it continues. In the rural areas, it is common place for the woman to forfeit her right of inheritance altogether. The custom of "*nayor*" is the right to visit her father's home once or twice a year. After marriage the woman will forfeit her right to her 'share of the inheritance to retain these rights. Even where she does not do this formally, in most cases, she is lucky if she gets more than a token of her share. This is despite the fact that in a family with a son and three daughters, the aggregate share of the daughters would be more than that of the sons. (It would be 1/5 for each daughter making a total of 3/5 for the girls as against 2/5 for the son.) However, in the case of marriage, the pronouncement is made that the daughter ceases to be part of her father's family.

The Family Laws Ordinance brought about one change that was even more fundamental than the possible changes advocated. The rule had been that where a child predeceased his or her parent, the grandchildren would not inherit. This rule had sometimes led to hardship and had been criticized. By the Ordinance, the grandchildren in such a case were made competent to inherit what their deceased parent would have inherited.

(b) Hindu women

Hindu women have very limited rights of inheritance in respect of their father's property. They can inherit only in five situations. The criterion for inheriting is the potential for providing a suitable male heir who could perform the funeral rites for the woman's parent. An unmarried daughter is an heir as the father is seen as having neglected his duty to get his daughter married. A widowed daughter with no sons or a married daughter past the age of childbearing cannot inherit. A woman is, however, entitled to inherit from her mother and would be able to claim the dowry (*stridhan*) settled on a Hindu bride at the time of her marriage which she got in lieu of inheriting from her father. However, the fact that the Dowry Prohibition Act does not exempt *stridhan* from its effect has resulted in serious economic hardship for Hindu women.

(c) Christian women

Christians are governed by the Succession Act 1925. No difference is made under the law of intestate succession between males and females though a sum is reserved for the widow which is the first charge on the estate. However, a testator has an unfettered discretion and may leave property as he or she wishes.

2. Employment

(a) Formal sector

In recent years economic circumstances have compelled large numbers of Bangladeshi women to join the public workforce. This trend, for years a common practice among landless, poor and female-headed rural households, where women play an active role in home-based and community agriculture, has extended to urban centres, where thousands of women are joining garment manufacturing and other industries to supplement family income or maintain dependants. While increased representation in the workforce should in principle improve the social and economic position of women, their quality of life has in fact diminished. Compelled by economic necessity to join the workforce, the majority of working women derive little sense of economic liberty as conceived in modern feminist terms.

This is because women employed in the formal sector face a variety of gender discrepancies in wage levels, social benefit entitlements and working conditions. Although steps have been taken to introduce egalitarian employment rights laws, these have had only modest impact on the situation of working women. Wage disparity in the garment industry, where women's income averages less than 84 per cent of that of men, is representative of women's situation throughout the formal industrial sector. While women in higher-level government and private sector positions are spared many of the physical discomforts faced by wage labourers, gender bias is reflected in salary and benefit disparities, incidents of sexual harassment, and a variety of impediments to women's advancement to senior positions.

Despite gradual progress towards the official quota of 15 per cent women's representation in government service, women remain significantly underrepresented, with a similar situation prevailing in the private sector and the professions. There are no women Secretaries, while only one of 80 Additional Secretaries is a woman. In the judicial service, women are modestly represented in the mid-level and magistrate ranks, but virtually absent from the senior judiciary. Women presently constitute only 24 per cent of the student body at the University of Dhaka. Only 1,000 women hold executive positions in the private sector, compared with over 300,000 men.

Although the mass entry of women into the workforce has effectively redefined the traditional social order, societal values defining women's marginal domestic status persist in undermining their equal participation in economic life. Social prejudices rooted in traditional cultural bias against women's economic activity outside the home continue to impose serious obstacles to women's economic empowerment. Women's increasing participation in the workforce has not been matched by sustained efforts to remove the traditional constraints on their economic activity imposed by social practices, laws, and policies regarding land rights, matrimonial property entitlements, and inheritance. For example, personal laws of inheritance constrain women's economic mobility and access to education. Perceptions of male authority impact on family support as well as government policies for the allocation of land and access to credit and other economic resources. Continued societal commitment to the notion of male dominance legitimizes male preferences and creates insensitivity to gender dimensions in social and economic relations, policy planning, and administrative decision making.

Persistent gender bias in economic affairs is in part attributable to the failure to use the law as an effective mechanism for improved gender equity. Laws and policies continue to marginalize women, ignoring women's contribution to family survival and the national economy. The interface between women's economic advancement and the personal laws that define their traditional roles have not been adequately addressed by policy planners. As a result, many of the progressive laws intended to protect the economic rights of women have ultimately had only marginal effect, failing to fulfil law's true potential in advancing women's economic rights. As a result, gender stereotyping and the inequalities which it condones undermine whatever gains are made by women's economic empowerment. For example, the egalitarian reform of certain employment laws has not been accompanied by corresponding enforcement efforts and policy interventions. Likewise, the economic activity of women heads of households are neglected by policy planners, who regard domestic and economic rights as separate and distinct areas of intervention.

(b) Informal sector

While women employed in the formal government and private sectors are subject to a variety of gender inequalities that inhibit their economic advancement, the situation of women in the informal sector is significantly worse. The informal sector, defined for these purposes as all income-generating processes which are not subject to regulatory rules or conditions, employs a large percentage of the working population of Bangladesh. In Dhaka, it is estimated to account for at least 66 per cent of the total labour force.

The informal sector attracts persons who lack the education and skills necessary for employment in the formal sector. It comprises a variety of subcategories of labour, including self-employed traders, artisans and craft producers; home-based producers of items on contract to industry; domestic servants; wage workers in general service, construction, and other fields; and temporary and casual labourers. The growth of the informal sector is attributable to a variety of supply and demand factors, including the number of persons compelled to accept employment in any circumstances, and the cost-reduction goals that motivate industries and commercial ventures that are technically part of the formal sector to establish informal labour pools to avoid minimum wage and social benefit responsibilities and maintain a flexible workforce to which retrenchment, collective bargaining or other legal conditions or responsibilities are attached.

A high concentration of women in the informal sector reflects a combination of barriers to women's access to the formal sector, including discriminatory attitudes concerning female employment; lower educational levels; limited mobility imposed by cultural norms; reproductive roles; and domestic responsibilities. Within the informal sector, women are particularly concentrated in garment manufacturing, food processing, and home-based production of piece-rate items on contract to industry or exploitative middlemen. With no recourse to minimum wage, social benefit, or other formal legal protections women in the informal sector face a variety of employment inequalities, including low and stagnant earnings; irregularity of work; physical hazards; lack of sanitation, child care and other facilities; unreasonably long hours; and aid-associated health risks.

Early marriage and divorce are a direct consequence of dowry demands. More than 20,000 marriages were terminated during the last five years in five thanas of Barguna district in Barisal division in south Bangladesh, the main reasons being dowry, polygamy and "immoral activity" of husbands. Parents also reportedly marry off their infant daughters to avoid paying higher dowry prices in the future. A recent study found that 50 per cent of the women in Bangladesh are married before the age of 16 while 98 per cent are married by the age of 24.

E. Violence against women

Gender-based violence is a form of discrimination that seriously inhibits women's constitutional rights to equality.

The Penal Code of Bangladesh which incorporated laws relating to violence including homicide and the causing of physical hurt, applied of course to both men and women. Some sections, however, pertain to acts of violence against women by "assault of criminal force to women to outrage her modesty", "kidnapping, abducting or inducing a woman to compel her into marriage" and rape. An increase in violence and growing protest by women's groups against this led to stronger punitive measures. The Cruelty to Women (Deterrent Punishment) Ordinance 1983 specifies life imprisonment for kidnapping or abducting, death for trafficking, dowry deaths and death or grievous hurt due to rape. This Act has been superseded by an even more draconian piece of legislation which provides the death penalty for rape even where it was not fatal. The poor enforcement of these laws, however, arises because the law enforcement institutions and agencies fail to recognize domestic violence and an unwillingness to intervene on behalf of the weak, the prevailing perception of women as subordinate acts as an impetus for violation of her human rights.

Marital rape is not recognized as an offence except where the wife is underage (see below).

1. Dowry-related violence

Dowry demands lead to other types of violence against women sometimes resulting in death. The following table documents dowry related violence reported in eight newspapers in Bangladesh from January to December 1995.

Table 1. Dowry-related violence reported in eight newspapers, January-December 1995

Nature of violence	Number of incidents	Number of police cases filed
Engagement broken	1	0
Physical torture	20	16
Physical torture & expelled from home	5	3
Sold to traffickers	1	0
Disappeared	1	1
Suicide	4	3
Threatened with death	2	1
Death	60	55
Total	**94**	**79**

These cases are of course only the reported ones. Many incidents of dowry-related violence remain as invisible as their victims.

Such cases continue to be reported despite legal prohibition against the taking of dowry. Under the Dowry Prohibition Act, 1980 (Dowry Act), as amended, the taking or giving of dowry, as well as demanding it, is punishable for not less than one year and not more than five years and/or a fine. As lawyers have found, the fact that both parties are punishable under the Dowry Act makes it less likely that a complaint will be filed, as even if one party is innocent, the other party may threaten to file a counter complaint.

Procedural flaws exist as well. Under the Dowry Act, offences are only cognizable if a complaint is filed with a first-class magistrate judge. This is in contrast to a normal criminal case which may be lodged with police. Because of this procedural requirement, those wishing to report a violation of the Dowry Act cannot do so at the local police station as the police have no jurisdiction. Rather, they most likely must employ the services of a lawyer familiar with the court system to register their complaint. Given that the victims of dowry demands are often very poor and the scarcity of attorneys handling such matters on a *pro bono* basis, it is not surprising that the number of complaints filed is small.

An additional special law was enacted to deter dowry-related violence: the Cruelty to Women (Deterrent Punishment) Ordinance (1983). Under this Ordinance, causing or attempting to cause death or grievous hurt to a woman for dowry is punishable with the following: (a) death; (b) life imprisonment; or (c) rigorous imprisonment for up to 14 years. As with other laws, the rate of arrest, prosecution and conviction under the Ordinance is unsatisfactory. However, as indicated by the newspaper reports above, dowry related violence continues despite the harsh penalties prescribed by the Ordinance. The enhancement of punishment under The Repression of Women and Children (Special Provisions) Act 1995 has not had the desired effect of reducing the number of such incidents of violence.

2. Rape

Rape of women is a daily occurrence in Bangladesh. Table 2 illustrates the occurrences of rapes as reported in eight newspapers:

Table 2. Rapes reported in eight Bangladesh newspapers, January-December 1995

	6–10 years	11–15 years	16–20 years	20+ years	Age not mentioned	Total
Gang rape	4	26	24	33	28	115
Rape by individual	19	14	6	7	11	57
Rape by police	1	4	5	2	4	16
Type of rape not mentioned	–	–	–	–	2	2

Source: Compiled by Ain-Salish Kendra, Documentation Unit, Bangladesh.

Note: In one case, the woman raped was pregnant. In five cases, others beside the victim died as a consequence of the rape (e.g. victim's relatives, witnesses, assisting police officer).

As in many other countries, social pressures on victims of rape to remain silent or blaming the victim for the rape are barriers to reporting cases to the police. However, even when these formidable barriers are crossed, the rate of arrest, prosecution, and conviction of rapists is small. One report stated that 40 per cent of cases of murder, dacoity and rape filed between 1990-1994 are still pending. Of 1,391 rape cases filed between 1990-1992, 445 cases or 31 per cent are still pending in 1995. Of 468 rape cases registered in 1990, a mere 29 per cent of the accused were convicted. One reason for the low rate of conviction may be the failure of the police to produce a charge sheet, a necessary step to pursue a case against the offender. In 1990, only 356 charge sheets were filed in a total of 468 rape cases. Delay in investigation or filing is especially detrimental in rape cases where physical evidence not properly taken and preserved may be lost forever.

Even more troubling, many cases of rape by police officers themselves have been reported, including the tragic case of Yasmeen Akhtar of Dinajpur.

Yasmeen's Case

On Thursday, 24 August 1995, 14-year-old Yasmeen Akhtar, a domestic servant working in Dhaka, was on her way home to the village of Ramnagar in Dinajpur, a district in north Bangladesh. At about 3.30 a.m., Yasmeen's bus reached the Dosh Mile bus stop where she would have to change buses. The bus driver asked the owner of a nearby *pan* shop to put her on the first bus to Dinajpur. A boy whom she met on the bus waited with her. At approximately 4 a.m., a police van with Dinajpur licence plates carrying three officers stopped at the Dosh Mile bus stop. The officers asked Yasmeen and her friend where they were going, and the two replied accordingly. The officer driving the van offered Yasmeen a ride, but she declined. The driver scolded her and made her get in the back of the van.

A few hours later, her body was found lying near her destination. The police in the van alleged that she jumped out of the speeding vehicle, but an autopsy later revealed that she had been raped and strangled to death.

After Yasmeen's rape, the people of Dinajpur and women throughout Bangladesh came together to protest violence against women and police-perpetrated violence. After national media attention, a case was filed against the officers responsible for Yasmeen's rape. Despite the high profile of this case, the trial has been postponed pending further investigation while Yasmeen's mother continues to be harassed by those who want her to dismiss the case. [Since this report was written the case has been heard and the major perpetrators have been convicted of murder.]

In addition to Yasmeen's case, earlier incidents of violence against women by police were reported in newspapers:

- In June, a young girl was raped in the Officer Commander's house, and a complaint was filed with the court in Haluarghat thana. On 4 August, the case against the officer was closed.

- On 10 September 1995, at 4 a.m. on a Friday morning, the Officer in Charge of Palashbari thana asked a woman who arrived on a night coach to come to the thana for her own security. She was raped by the Officer in Charge of the station. He was arrested.

- A police constable was given seven years imprisonment and fined 3,000 takas by a District Judge for attempting to rape a six-year-old girl.

The Bangladesh Penal Code of 1875 and two special laws, the Cruelty to Women (Deterrent Punishment) Ordinance 1983 and the Oppression Against Women and Children Ordinance 1995, define and punish rape. The special laws supersede the Penal Code. However, cases are still being brought under the Penal Code. The Penal Code defines rape as follows:

A man is said to commit "rape" who, except in the case hereinafter excepted, has sexual intercourse with a woman under circumstances falling under any of the five following descriptions:

First	Against her will.
Secondly	Without her consent.
Thirdly	With her consent, when her consent has been obtained by putting her in fear of death, or of hurt.
Fourthly	With her consent, when the man knows that he is not her husband, and that her consent is given because she believes that he is another man to whom she is or believes herself to be lawfully married.
Fifthly	With or without her consent, when she is under 16 years of age.
Explanation	Penetration is sufficient to constitute the sexual intercourse necessary to the offence of rape.
Exception	Sexual intercourse by a man with his own wife, the wife not being under 16 years of age, is not rape. (Bangladesh Penal Code 1875 (as amended)).

Thus, marital rape, even with the passage of two special laws on rape, remains legal unless the victim is under 16.

The most significant difference between the three laws are in the sentencing provisions, as illustrated in table 3:

Table 3. Comparison of rape sentencing provisions

Offence committed	Penal code	Cruelty to women ordinance 1983	Oppression against women & children ordinance 1995
Rape	Life imprisonment or maximum 10 years imprisonment and fine	n.a.	Death or life imprisonment
Death caused while committing rape	n.a.	Death or life imprisonment & fine (applies to attempted rapes as well)	Death
Rape and culpable homicide	n.a.	Death or life imprisonment & fine	Death
Death following rape	n.a.	n.a.	Death or life imprisonment
Rape and attempted culpable homicide	n.a.	Life imprisonment or max. 14 years imprisonment & fine	Death or life imprisonment
Rape and grievous hurt	n.a.	Life imprisonment or max. 14 years imprisonment & fine	Death or life imprisonment
Gang rape or death following gang rape	n.a.	n.a.	Death or life imprisonment

The effectiveness of the severe punishments provided for in the law, especially the death penalty, are questionable. First, legal literacy is very low in Bangladesh, even among law enforcement officials. Most people will not adjust their behaviour because they fear severe punishment when they are unaware of such punishment. Second, the harsh mandatory sentences and lack of flexibility in sentencing may result in judicial reluctance to convict under this law. The mandatory sentences may also discourage law enforcement personnel from charging persons under this Ordinance to avoid acquittal, among other reasons. Finally, human rights groups have criticized the use of the death penalty as a violation of fundamental rights, and have argued that when it is legal, it should be carefully circumscribed, not used as a blanket remedy to combat criminal behaviour.

The rather cavalier use of the death penalty in attempts to reform laws applying to violence against women is a band aid remedy to serious and pervasive problems.

A project entitled Violence Free Cities investigated enforcement of the 1995 Act in two thanas (urban administrative units) in Dhaka and found that police officers tend to file cases that would fall under the Act under other laws, such as the general Penal Code. The reasons for this are many. First, police may not be aware of the 1995 Act. Second, they may file a charge under the Penal Code because of its less severe sentencing provisions. Finally, corruption may be a factor.

Enacting ever increasingly harsh sentencing provisions without reform of police investigation procedures and evidentiary requirements and educating law enforcement personnel has proved ineffective. Defects in the system which occur before sentencing must be addressed.

3. Fatwa

Salish (mediation) is a traditional form of arbitration. The arbiters are usually the local elite (village elders, school master, Imam and so on). Both sides should be represented. In practice a woman is discouraged from presenting her side. The decision given at the *salish* is not legally binding and no method of enforcing the judgment exists. Many case studies state that despite an adverse *salish* decision the losing party refused to part with her/his land or to pay any fine that may have been imposed. Alongside *salish* for the settlement of disputes, village councils also meet of their own initiative to accuse individuals (mainly women) of misbehaviour and "sentence" them to a variety of punishments, based on customary practices. A fatwa is an opinion given by an Islamic scholar in response to a question involving a point of law.

Increasingly, fatwas are being used to bolster the authority of the *salish* and the Imam. Pronounced by people who have no legal authority, they do not clarify an ambiguous legal situation but weigh up evidence which traditionally was never a function of a fatwa giver. Sometimes, fatwas are being given by the wrong person, in the wrong circumstances and for the wrong purposes.

The following is a sample of the types of fatwas issued against women.

Against contraceptive use:

June 1993:	35 women in a village in Serajgong ostracized for using contraceptives.
November 1993:	Two imams were suspended from their mosque duties because their wives used contraceptives.

Against education:

January 1995:	Children deterred from going to schools run by Bangladesh Rural Advancement Committee (BRAC), a development NGO. Imams refused to perform burial rites for children attending BRAC schools.
February 1995:	Schools burned following fatwas.

Against women's development:

January 1994:	600 mulberry trees cultivated by women cut down by Madrassah students.
March 1994:	10 women divorced for working with NGOs and ostracized for working outside the home.

F. Conclusion

It has been said that violence against women is the most pervasive abuse of human rights. Women have been victims of violence within the family, in the community and by the state agencies. In Bangladesh there are indications of a steady increase in violence against women. A woman victim of violence faces an apathetic family, especially in cases of domestic violence, she confronts grossly insensitive law-enforcing and judicial agencies such as the police and court officials, and experiences difficulties in accessing the medical service for treatment and for notification in defence of her case. When her security is at stake, she does not find a safe shelter or a means of livelihood for herself and her children. The multidimensional character of violence is thus evident.

Over the years, concern with the status of women in Bangladesh has led successive governments to undertake programmes to alleviate their situation. While the emphasis shifted from social welfare to skill development and self-employment, these initiatives highlighted the necessity of ensuring a proper atmosphere for women to participate in socio-economic activities. A more comprehensive approach to the integration of women in national development is advocated.

It is important to understand the multidimensional nature of violence experienced by women, women's resistance and coping strategies both at the individual and at the collective level, and the nature of formal and informal interventions made to combat and oppose violence. Implications of social assumptions of women's role in the family and society impact on the legal and judicial understanding of the problem and thereby influence the strategies that are proposed. Thus, we need to be clear that violence against women is systemic and the physical brutalization of woman is only one manifestation of endemic societal violence. Where society itself is unequal and unjust it is perpetuating a cycle of injustice. Both men and women are its victims because in a society which is essentially unjust there are, in the long run, no winners.

AN UPDATE

The Bangladesh government, in its declaration of National Policy on Women (dated 8 March 1997) identified actions against violence as a priority area for intervention. The Policy focused on eradication of physical, mental and sexual harassment at the family and social levels; forced prostitution of women and rape; dowry; and violence against women. It proposed amendments of existing laws which are repressive to women and formulation of new laws. The Policy recommended special assistance in incidents of rape and trafficking of women and children. Further, it recommended participation of women in the judicial and police service and proposed simpler legal and judicial procedures.

Similarly the draft 55-year-plan has identified elimination of all sorts of violence against women. The plan identified the elimination of all discriminatory laws, rules, regulations and practices governing the family, social, cultural, economic and political aspects of life as a strategic means to achieve women in development goals.

III. CAMBODIA*

A. Introduction

Cambodia is among the 10 poorest countries in the world, with a GDP per capita of US$ 200. More than half of its 10.7 million population are women. They represent 52 per cent of the population. One in four households is headed by women, the result of Cambodia's war-ravaged history. Yet in spite of the fact that women disproportionately outnumber men in the labour force, the generally low literacy level among Cambodian women and traditional social attitudes has meant that there has been little progress made in the strengthening of women's rights in the public and private spheres. The status of women in Cambodian society remains low.

B. Constitutional guarantees

Within the provisions of the Constitution of the Kingdom of Cambodia (1993) human rights as defined in the Universal Declaration of Human Rights (1948) and other international instruments related to human rights, women and children's rights are recognized and respected (Article 31). Specific provisions with regard to women include the right of equal pay for equal work, the right to take maternity leave with full pay and no loss of seniority or other social benefits (Articles 36 and 46). Implementation of these constitutional provisions into domestic law has been slow. Where actions have been taken to bring domestic laws into line with the Constitution, such as in the promulgation of a new Labour Law in early 1997, specific provisions to provide women in the labour force with social protection such as maternity benefits fall short of the international standard adopted in the Constitution. For example, in Cambodia, women workers are entitled to receive only half their pay as benefits during maternity leave.

C. Cambodian women's code

Since 1994, Cambodia has worked on a Women's Code which aims to consolidate laws relating to labour, crimes and other laws that pertain to women. The Code had not been completed by March 1996, as reported at the fifty-second session of the United Nations Economic and Social Council.

---

* This paper is based on materials submitted by Serey Phal KIEN, President, Cambodian Women's Development Association.

D. Some critical areas of discrimination faced
by Cambodian women

The legal and regulatory machinery in Cambodia is weak. Where laws do exist, enforcement is difficult, if not totally non-existent. This situation, together with women's low literacy and the prevailing socio-cultural norms which render women subservient to men, restricts their access to information on their human rights in areas which have particular relevance to their daily lives, such as reproductive rights, domestic violence, sexual violence and forced prostitution and sex trafficking.

1. Reproductive rights

The lack of laws to provide legal protection and assistance to women in the exercise of their rights to have control over and to decide freely and responsibly on matters related to their sexuality is a problem. Owing to cultural barriers and a general taboo on issues concerning sexuality and reproductive health, Cambodian women are prevented from seeking information and advice on these concerns. The lack of public education programmes offered to women, especially in rural areas, on subjects related to the human anatomy, sexuality and reproductive health, including birth spacing and birth control, results in unwanted pregnancies. Many urban and rural poor women still do not have access to birth control programmes or to birth control contraceptives and other devices. Or, where such programmes may exist, the prohibitive cost of certain birth control contraceptives and devices for most low income families rules out their use. In other cases, where birth control drugs or devices have been distributed, the inadequate monitoring and control of these programmes has led to both real and perceived illeffects of the drugs and devices and has raised generalized fears among the population at large concerning the safety of such birth control methods and devices.

The prevailing socio-cultural norms, which place men in a dominant role in marriage and in the family, assign to their wives (sometimes under threat of violence) the role of providing for the sexual needs and comfort of their husbands. The general view held is that it is the responsibility of the wife to find ways to prevent pregnancy as childbearing is more her concern than that of her husband. Thus, husbands may refuse to cooperate in the application of birth control measures where they believe or perceive that such a method will reduce or inhibit their sexual pleasure. In some cases, husbands have applied physical beatings, psychological abuse and sexual assaults and rape against their wives where they believe their wives have deviated from the above-stated culturally accepted view that it is a wife's duty to satisfy the sexual needs of her husband. The lack of public education programmes aimed at changing the attitudes and practices of men will only perpetuate the difficulties of women in this area.

2. Domestic violence

Of all the security issues affecting Cambodian women, it is the problem of wife abuse in the family which is the most pervasive. While no accurate statistics are available, authorities interviewed during a pilot study on domestic violence in 1994 estimated that the most serious cases of wife abuse in the family – resulting in death or severe injury, occurred in approximately 25 per cent of households. Even the authorities themselves consider this estimate to be low, since it is based on complaints received or serious cases brought to their attention.

Apart from the obvious victims of wife battering, the far larger number of domestic violence victims are women who regularly and continuously suffer from various forms of physical beatings, psychological abuse, sexual assaults and economic deprivations by their husbands, but who do not report these acts to the authorities due, in part, to fear of reprisals from their spouses. There are also cases of incest where second husbands, having agreed to marry divorced or widowed women, claim the right to take the virginity of their daughters, having missed the virginity of their wives.

Husbands and other male members of the household are the usual perpetrators of violence, while women and children, especially daughters, are the overwhelming victims. Domestic violence cuts across all social classes. It is not only women who are economically dependent on their husbands who are at risk of being abused. Women family breadwinners are also included.

Deeply rooted socio-cultural norms perpetuate gender inequality and create the basis for domestic violence. This stems from childhood, where children are brought up to believe that the husband is the head of the household and the wife's role is to ensure the comfort of her husband and to bear and care for his children. This is carried over into adulthood, where wives are constantly reminded by their parents, friends, other women and the authorities that inadequate fulfilment of their comfort-giving and caretaking roles in the home is a breach of their responsibility to their husbands. They should do their best to satisfy their husbands if they do not want to be beaten. In Cambodia, the lack of education and understanding in the community about the cycle of domestic violence results in the continued acceptance of violence by women from their husbands. Due to the lack of sympathy and support, both real and perceived, by their family members and society at large, wives often believe that they have no recourse against such violence and that they must stay and accept the violence, usually blaming themselves and/or attributing her suffering to fate or "karma".

Victims of domestic violence often do not have adequate recourse to legal redress and the protection of state authorities. This is because wife battering is considered a private family matter by the courts, the police and local authorities. Women are therefore counselled to be patient and tolerant while their abusers go unpunished. Where there are existing provisions within the law dealing with marital issues, these tend to minimize any assault or beating, short of extensive physical harm or death, and effectively preclude any hope of an immediate remedy to protect a woman suffering from abuse and battering. Furthermore, the legal system and court procedures are often ill-equipped to protect women in such cases. The overwhelming majority of judges are male, and few have been trained in gender sensitivity. This is further compounded by the lack of legal, health and social services.

In the absence of a law on domestic violence, the legal system cannot provide women with the protection and assistance they seek to bring an end to such violence. Only the most heinous acts of violence or those that result in death are considered by the courts and then only as grounds for divorce. Legal divorce proceedings which include mandatory reconciliation referrals without provision for the protection of victims of domestic violence highlight the inadequacies in the existing family laws. Moreover, legal divorce proceedings themselves take too long to offer any effective relief and protection for the victim of abuse. These inadequacies in the law render the state authorities, and law offices helpless. Another problem area is the corruption of some authorities which serves to negate any effective legal protection to woman victims of domestic abuse.

3. Trafficking and prostitution of women

Prostitution is not new in Cambodia, especially in the period 1970-1975, when social problems caused by worsening civil war facilitated its growth. During the Khmer Rouge years, prostitution was completely banned and eliminated. But the problem reared its head again after the ouster of the Khmer Rouge in 1979. During the 1980s the number of prostitutes was estimated to be 7,000-8,000 throughout the whole country.

After the arrival of the United Nations Transitional Authority in Cambodia (UNTAC), which suddenly arrived in Cambodia, prostitution grew dramatically again, not only in Phnom Penh but in all major provincial towns. By the end of 1992, the number of prostitutes in Phnom Penh alone was estimated at between 8,000 and 10,000. However, what has been alarming is that the age of prostitutes has declined. Surveys conducted by the Cambodian Women's Development Association showed that, while the minimum age of prostitutes was 18 years in October 1992, it had dropped to 15 years by April 1993. Currently, girls as young as 12 or 13 years can be seen working in the sex industry. Surveys also revealed that 35 per cent of prostitutes were under the age of 18. The actual number of children engaged in prostitution could be much higher than recorded in surveys (as the surveys themselves are conducted only in places where prostitution is practised openly).

The surveys also confirmed the rise in the abduction or deception of women and children for the sale to brothels. Forty-eight per cent of prostitutes had been sold to brothels. Compounding the problem is the smuggling in and out of the country of women and children by international sex traders. The problem of sex trafficking in Cambodia does not only concern Cambodian women and children, but also Vietnamese, Thai and Chinese women and children who are brought into Cambodia for prostitution. It is most likely that many of them will also be trafficked onto other countries (through Cambodia).

Most prostitutes do not wish to join the sex trade but would prefer to have another job, if given a chance. Poverty and deception (particularly by people they trust) were cited as the main reasons for their being in the trade. About one quarter of women and girls, having been sold to their first owner, face the likelihood of being sold on to another country later. The rest will eventually be sold on to another brothel owner in the same area or in another province. The prices fetched in the trading of women and girls depend on the physical attributes of the individual woman or girl, namely her virginity, age and beauty. Although the problem is still in its early stages, having appeared in its more organized form only within the past two to three years, prostitution and trafficking in women and children are spreading fast. Despite the rapid growth of this problem, there are still no clear policies or programmes to deal with it.

The inadequacy of the laws and the legal system to provide protection to women in the sex industry has meant that women are punished and harassed by law enforcement officials rather than those who wield control over the women, the brothel owners, agents, procurers, pimps and customers, who go unpunished. Corruption within the law enforcement institutions further weakens the position of women sex workers to seek legal redress. Although a law on the kidnapping and trafficking of women is being drafted, no legal mechanisms currently exist to combat sex trafficking. And those mechanisms and procedures within the existing laws that could be used in combatting the trafficking of women remain under-utilized.

The above situation has given rise to several serious violations of the human and health rights of women sex workers. The rights of women sex workers are compromised when clients insist on unprotected sex (often with threats made by the brothel owner) which expose the women to HIV/AIDS and other sexually transmitted diseases (STDs). Refusal of the demands of their clients usually means harsh measures, including various forms of physical and mental torture, which can be in the form of beatings by brothel owners with electric wires, electric shock and forced confinement in locked dark rooms. Some women have been beaten to death. The forced intake of drugs so that they may service their clients is included among the inhuman treatment meted out to women sex workers by their employers. Forced sex even during menstruation and sickness, the forcing of women to undergo unhygenic and dangerous surgical procedures to resew their hymens in order to create the illusion that they are virgins, the freedom of male workers at the brothel to rape a woman sex worker after she has been sold to the first client as well as rape by local authorities without payment constitute some of the acts which violate the personal security and bodily integrity of these women. Moreover, they face economic exploitation. They are required to work long hours without rest and with half of their income taken by their brothel owners. In the absence of medical care for the treatment of STDs and HIV/AIDS being provided by their employers, should they contract HIV/AIDS or any other STD, they may face banishment from the brothel.

Aside from the inadequacy of the law, there are also social factors which have a detrimental effect on the rights of women sex workers and respect for their human rights. These social barriers include the stereotyping of women as providers of pleasure to men, a role that is reinforced by the media, the unequal access of women to education which results in the marginalization of some women to work in prostitution and societal ostracism of commercial sex workers, which makes it difficult for them to seek assistance for health and security reasons.

4. Sexual assault and rape

Violence against women exists in many forms. It is found in the home in the form of marital rape and incest (including rape by a stepfather). It is in the schools where the sexual solicitation and rape of girl students by teachers and other school authorities and the sexual harassment of and solicitation of female teachers is known. Sexual violence is also found in the workplace in all sectors: government establishments, in the private sector and also in the informal sector, including domestic workers. In the rural countryside of Cambodia, sexual assault and rape of rural women by government and Khmer Rouge soldiers, as well as by bandits, is well known. It exists among the poor and destitute – homeless women and women squatters, with little in terms of civil status – who are often most vulnerable. Violence against women exists at all levels of society. Given the social attitudes in Cambodia, and the inherent discrimination of the legal system, a victim of sexual violence often finds her role changes from that of a complainant to a defendant as she is required to prove she did not invite the harassment and assault to law enforcers, the court, the community, to her family and prospective husband. The socially induced shame and societal ostracism prevents women and girl victims from actively pursuing redress of their grievances. Victims often simply choose to suffer privately.

IV. FIJI

THE LEGAL STATUS OF FIJI WOMEN*

A. Introduction

The de jure and de facto constitutional and legal status of women in Fiji reflects and reinforces women's discriminatory social, cultural, political and economic position. Discrimination against women occurs in the legislation and in the form of interpretative and procedural legal discrimination in the Courts of law and law enforcement agencies. Even when there is formal legal equality, discriminatory interpretation of the legislation often has harsh consequences for women.

The legalistic form of the law espouses the application of the principle of formal legal equality. That is, it applies abstract legal principles without distinction or qualification to all people. Formal legal equality assumes that all disputants who seek justice are, in fact, equal before the law. There is a commonplace belief that the law is gender-neutral, that "justice is blind" and that the law affects men and women similarly.[1]

The endurance of this notion has meant that the structure and content of the law has rarely been questioned. The notion does not take into account that women are severely economically and socially disadvantaged and cannot "compete" on the same terms as men. The notion that all persons are "equal" before the law is farcical and is depicted in a cartoon in which three elderly male justices are seen looking down with astonishment at their very pregnant bellies. One justice says to the other, "Perhaps we'd better reconsider that decision".[2]

Although poor people in general are affected by the law, women are particularly disadvantaged as they more often have less access to information about legislation and laws that affect them than men and are less able to afford legal representation and services. Women are therefore doubly disadvantaged because of their gender.[3]

While the law provides a powerful source for the shaping of gender ideology, it is by no means the cause of gender inequalities. Rather, a particular interpretation of the law, both written and unwritten, reinforces an already existing gender inequality, to strengthen and

---

* By P. Imrana Jalal, Pacific Regional Human Rights Education Resource Team, British Aid (RRRT), Fiji.

[1] P. I. Jalal, *Pacific Women and the Law: A Legal Rights Handbook,* Fiji Women's Rights Movement, 1996.

[2] Susan M. Okin, *Justice, Gender and the Family*, Basic Books, 1989.

[3] International Women's Tribune Centre Newsletter, *Women and the Law*, July 1990, p. 45.

perpetuate discrimination against women. A legislative strategy may address some expressions of gender inequality and seek to confront some of the underlying institutional foundations. It is not possible to legislate allegiance to non-discriminatory attitudes. This requires changes in social and cultural attitudes. However, the law has an important role to play in addressing the discrimination that women face in general; in acting as a catalyst for change; in hastening a change in cultural and social attitudes and in allowing individual women and groups of women to use the law to obtain just solutions.

Laws are not monolithic and intransigent. They are shaped by political and socio-economic developments and are concerned with an evolving selection of customs, traditions, religious codes and external sources of law. Together with their interpretations and applications, the laws shape and influence women's socialization, education, employment, marriage, exercise of sexuality and social and political participation.

Legal discrimination is not always apparent from reading legislation. Legislation that appears to be theoretically fair or gender-neutral in its written form may, in fact, produce a discriminatory effect. Discrimination may therefore occur either directly or indirectly.

Direct discrimination occurs when men are given rights which women are denied and this is apparent from a reading of the legislation without reference to external sources to assist in the particular law's interpretation. Indirect discrimination occurs when women are discriminated against in comparison to men because the Courts and law agencies do not take into account women's disadvantaged economic, social and political position when applying, interpreting or enforcing the written laws. These laws are written in a gender-neutral form. The law in this regard discriminates against women in its effect. In this respect the law does not take cognizance of external matters relating to women which have a discriminatory impact on women's status.

Procedural and interpretative discrimination occurs when the Courts, law enforcement agencies and law-associated agencies interpret and enforce laws and procedures in ways which discriminate against women because of particular social and cultural attitudes about women's behaviour. These attitudes are not apparent when the law is applied to men. In this regard the law has a discriminatory effect on women. This form of discrimination is a form of indirect discrimination.

The law may also be discriminatory where it fails to intervene to correct women's discriminatory status. Here, affirmative action laws and policies become significant in addressing the imbalances.

There are two models utilized by tribunals in assessing what constitutes discrimination. One model is that of the "similarity and difference test". This test of discrimination uses the male standard of equality. Women are then put in a position of having to argue that they are the same as men and should be treated the same, or that they are different and should be treated the same or that they are different and should be afforded special treatment. This model of discrimination does not allow for questioning the ways in which laws or cultures or social traditions have constructed and maintained the disadvantage of women, or the extent to which institutions are male-defined.

A second test of discrimination, as adopted by the Supreme Court of Canada[4] determines discrimination in terms of disadvantage. If a person is a member of a particularly disadvantaged group and can show that a law, policy or behaviour maintains or worsens that disadvantage, it is discriminatory. No comparator is required. The "disadvantage" model of discrimination captures the systemic nature of discrimination against women and is more consistent with the object and purpose of the United Nations Convention on the Elimination of All Forms of Discrimination Against Women (CEDAW, the "Women's Convention").

In order to comprehend the impact of discriminatory laws on women's lives a broader understanding of the economic, social and political conditions of women's lives is required.

B. The general status of Fiji women

Women comprise half of Fiji's population, estimated at the end of 1993 to be 771,104. Despite these large numbers, women as a group reap few of the benefits of development and endure more of the drawbacks. Females are less likely than males to be educated and less likely to proceed to tertiary education. This is so despite their higher achievement levels at school than males. They are less likely to obtain well-paid jobs and to obtain promotions than males. They own fewer businesses and obtain less credit. Females are significantly under-represented in leadership positions and senior positions in government. Females are overwhelmingly the victims of violence and make up the largest numbers of the unemployed and poor.[5] They also suffer from legal discrimination in the criminal law, family law and under the Constitution of Fiji.

Recent years have seen rising unemployment and poverty, a growing dependence of women on wage employment, a rising level of female-headed households and the erosion of living standards. The number of families receiving financial family assistance through the Department of Social Welfare has increased from 5,166 in 1987 to 7,972 in 1993. Of these, 70 per cent are female-headed households. Twelve per cent of families receiving assistance have been deserted by male-breadwinner husbands or fathers. In 1992, there were 287 cases of maintenance and 179 applications for affiliation orders filed by women in the Suva Domestic Court. There were also 501 applications for warrants of non-payment of maintenance filed by women.[6]

Of some 3,000 applications received by the Poverty Alleviation Fund a year, of 609 projects granted funds, 432 projects were granted to men, whilst 149 were granted to women.[7]

---

[4] *Andrews v Law Society of Canada* (1989) 1 SCR 143.

[5] *Women of Fiji: A Statistical Gender Profile*, Department of Women and Culture, Fiji, 1994, pp. 1-2.

[6] Ibid., p. 57.

[7] *Fiji Business Review*, August 1993.

1. Political status and land rights

Traditionally, political power in indigenous Fijian society has been held by men and chiefly titles have usually been the domain of men except in the case of the extinction of the male line.[8] Political power for women is also intrinsically tied up with control over land.

Historically, the Native Lands Commission (NLC), supported by the Colonial Government strengthened matrilineal transfers of land. This meant that the Native Lands Commission with the support of the colonial Government formalised a matrilineal and patriarchal system of land management and control. This occurred despite the fact that some areas in Fiji were matrilineal. The Colonial Government dealt mostly with men in their dealings with locals and accepted and supported a male perspective of custom which reflected their own cultural values about women.

Land ownership of native land now defines ownership primarily in terms of matrilineal descent through the Constitution and Native Lands Act, Cap 133. Women did, however, upon the introduction of statutory law, become registered owners of native land based on their birthright as members of their *mataqali* or on registration. The *mataqali* is a landowning unit consisting of members of a clan, according to Fijian custom. Although the legislation is apparently gender-neutral and not discriminatory, because it purports to make women and men equal within the *mataqali*, women effectively have little control over land[9] as land rights are determined according to customary law.

Under this system, women cannot broadly convey or pass on their rights to land. When a woman from one *mataqali* marries a man from another *mataqali*, her children only have *vasu* rights to the land. *Vasu* rights are rights inherited through the mother but vasu rights have been weakening over generations. Her children do not have legal rights to the land held by their mother, which she owns communally with other members of her *mataqali*. However, they do have rights over their father's land in his *mataqali*. One way of putting it is that a child can sell the lease of his father's land but not a lease of his mother's land.

Indigenous women's rights to land are determined or influenced by their status and whether or not they have contributed to or worked the land in any way. It is not a simple task to gain ownership as many villages will not allow women to work the land. Women generally only hold usufruct rights to the land. Men therefore have full control and management over the land and women can only use, not control, the land. Women in traditional settings never have rights to home sites. This right belongs to their fathers or brothers. Women did not and do not generally give evidence in land claims of native owned lands as expert witnesses on customary law. The Native Lands Act and the Native Lands Commission determines rights to land by native customs and traditions which are largely defined by men.[10] A different outcome might be possible if women were used more as expert witnesses in Native Lands Commission hearings.

---

[8] C. Bolabola, *Fiji: Customary Constraints and Legal Progress in Land Rights of Pacific Women*, University of the South Pacific, 1986, pp. 4-6.

[9] Ibid., pp. 15-16.

[10] Ibid., p. 14.

Article 100 of the 1990 Fiji Constitution determines that customary law becomes part of the law of Fiji unless Parliament provides otherwise. By incorporation, the law favours males because custom provides that chiefly titles are held through the male line, although women do hold some titles in very isolated cases. If a woman who holds a title dies, her right is given to her closest male relative on her father's side. Generally, chiefly titles are inherited, as with land, through the male line and the Constitution reinforces this discrimination by formally recognizing customary law.

The lack of power that women had in traditional society has carried over into modern-day society. Despite the great strides that Fiji women have made in leadership positions and politics, there is a long way to go before there is bona fide power-sharing between men and women. In the 1994 general election, three Fijian women were elected to the House of Representatives, an increase from one woman in the 1992 election. Of 34 appointed members of Senate, three are women, all indigenous Fijian, all appointed by the Great Council of Chiefs. None of the President's nominees are women. Fijian women comprise five of the 51 members of the Great Council of Chiefs.

At the local government level, 21 women (mainly Fijian and only four Indo-Fijians) stood for election in 1993. Of these, six women were successful, none of whom were Indo-Fijian. The representation of women in appointed statutory boards is low. Females make up 14 per cent of non-position membership on boards and 13 per cent of all members. Position members are those who hold membership on boards by virtue of their positions in government and the private sector. At a national level, only 4 per cent of Tribunal members are women, 4 per cent of Commission members and 9 per cent of wages councils. The Judicial and Legal Services Commission and the Public Service Commission are significant in that they have no female members at all despite the fact that both Commissions affect large numbers of women.[11] There are currently no female judges or magistrates, although significantly, the Director of Public Prosecutions is female.

Overall, indigenous Fijian women have accessed the public realm more successfully than Indo-Fijian women, mainly because Fijian women have access through traditional chiefly power.

In order to influence leadership within government and society and the political process, there needs to be a critical mass of women, that is, larger numbers of women, in order to make a difference for women as a group.

Women's political participation in civil society has been minimal overall but during the period 1987 to 1995 there has been increased participation mainly through non-governmental organizations (NGOs).

Most women's NGOs are racially based and have mobilized on the basis of traditional activities. There are two loosely grouped types of women's NGOs in Fiji. The first type, such as the indigenous chiefly backed Soqosoqo Vakamarama and the Indo-Fijian TISI Sangam women's organization are the traditional, racial and rural-based NGO. The main

---

[11] *Women of Fiji: A Statistical Gender Profile*, pp. 3-7.

concerns of such groups are the welfare of women within the ethnic and customary context.[12] These groups thus concentrate on home development and traditional arts and crafts activities.

The second type of NGO, such as the Fiji Women's Rights Movement and the Women's Crisis Centre tend to be more multiracial and are committed to more progressive, non-traditional issues such as improving women's legal, political, social, cultural and economic status. The multiracial Fiji Women's Rights Movement successfully agitated during the election of 1987 to get all political parties to include and address women's issues in their election campaigns.

The umbrella NGO, the National Council of Women has tended to be conservative and works closely with the Department of Women. However, it has recently become involved in a project to encourage and train more women to become involved in politics. The Department of Women has in the past primarily supported the Soqosoqo Vakamarama and the National Council of Women. Both organizations enjoy excellent relations with both the government and the powerful Fijian hierarchy. In recent times the Department has given some minor support to multiracial women's NGOs such as the Fiji Women's Rights Movement.

The Indo-Fijian women's NGOs rarely participate in public affairs or comment on women's or other political issues. However the Fiji Girmit Council of Women, together with the National Federation Party Women's Wing, has for the first time recently during 1995 spoken out publicly, encouraging Indo-Fijian women to get more involved in public affairs and politics. The trade unions have active women's wings and the Young Women's Christian Organization is beginning to attract more Indo-Fijian women, although its membership is largely still Fijian.

C. Constitutional status

1. General rights and freedoms

Article 13 of the Fiji Constitution guarantees all Fiji citizens freedom of speech. Article 13 (2) (d) makes an exception to this fundamental freedom by attempting to limit freedom of speech to protect the "reputation, dignity and esteem of institutions and values of the Fijian people in particular the Bose Levu Vakaturaga (BLV)...". Although this is a general limitation on freedom of speech for all citizens, this limitation has distinct implications for women. This is because it may prevent women from challenging traditional customary laws and practices that discriminate against women. Fijian women are effectively gagged from challenging anything discriminatory that is legitimized under the mantle of custom. Such a provision therefore encourages the continuation of traditional patriarchal practices.

All women, but particularly indigenous Fijian women face indirect discrimination in terms of access to power and leadership in the Senate, the House of Representatives and in relation to the post of President.

---

[12]   E. Huffer, "Women and politics in the South Pacific", unpublished paper for the Fiji Women's Rights Movement and The Asia Foundation, 1993.

The President is appointed by the BLV. The BLV is mainly composed of indigenous men of chiefly rank. This provision is therefore indirectly discriminatory to all men and women of non-indigenous background but also to Fijian women, particularly commoner women. Given that women only make up small percentages of the BLV this effectively prevents them from aspiring to the highest Constitutional office.

In a similar manner, indigenous commoner women and non-Fijian men and women are indirectly excluded from Senate representation since membership to this body is by appointment of the BLV or the President. Twenty have to be indigenous Fijians appointed by the BLV and the President, one Rotuman to be appointed by the President and the Rotuma Island Council and nine others to be appointed exclusively by the President. It is noteworthy that although Fijian women comprise five of the 51 members of the BLV, of these three have been appointed by the BLV to the Senate. This does not, however, guarantee future female representation in the Senate. On the other hand, the President is not restricted by race, class or gender in his appointments but none of the President's appointees are women.

In other respects, the Constitution denies indigenous women full equality with men because of the selection of candidates for the House of Representatives through the provincial councils, which are heavily male-dominated. The current system of provincial representation promotes the selection of males as candidates to the House of Representatives because women are usually not members of provincial councils and decision-making bodies. Although the Constitutional provisions governing selection are theoretically gender-neutral because selection occurs through such bodies, indigenous women suffer indirect discrimination in the election process.

It is difficult to legislate to counteract such indirect discrimination. In this respect, changes in attitudes are more significant than the law. However, it is possible with affirmative action legislation, reserved parliamentary representation and female quotas to guarantee more female representation in legislative bodies.

2. Anti-discrimination provisions

Article 16 of the 1990 Constitution makes discrimination in general unlawful. It states that no law shall make any provision that is discriminatory either of itself or in its effect. The provision therefore provides against both direct and indirect sexual discrimination as the definition of "discrimination" includes sexual discrimination. "Sexual" discrimination was notably missing from the 1970 Constitution. Since 1990 any form of discrimination based on sex or gender is *prima facie* illegal. However, women's actual legal status in Fiji after the creation of the 1990 Constitution remains exactly the same. Theoretically, the onus rests on Fiji's Parliament to amend all laws which are now inconsistent with the 1990 Constitution.

3. Patrilineal Constitution

Despite the fact that some Fijian groups are matrilineal, the Fiji Constitution only legally recognizes patrilineal rights. The Fiji Native Lands Commission has acknowledged that "there are different customs for different provinces of Fiji governing the rules concerning the rights of a person to choose to be a member of either his mother's or his father's unit".[13]

---

[13]   *Women of Fiji: A Statistical Gender Profile*, p. 12.

The Constitution states that a legitimate child's rights are inherited through the father, not the mother. If a child is illegitimate, the child may claim citizenship and other rights through the mother.

Article 156 of the Constitution of Fiji states that a person shall be regarded as a Fijian, Indian or Rotuman only if that person's father is a Fijian, Indian or Rotuman. This provision produces iniquitous results for the children of mixed marriages in terms of, among many things, scholarship rights and jobs in the civil service. The children of Fijian women married to non-Fijian men are therefore discriminated against.

The recognition of patrilineal rights in the Constitution also has special application to indigenous Fijian women whose customary law status has been legitimized by the Constitution, which legally discriminates against them in respect of who is entitled to be "Fijian".

All indigenous persons are entitled to be registered in the *Vola ni Kawa Bula*. Registration entitles a person to claim rights to Fijian native land, to stand for election in the racially based national legislature, to obtain profits from native leases, to obtain special scholarship privileges and to be entitled to special affirmative action benefits. Registration is based on being able to prove that a person's father is a Fijian. Thus children born of indigenous women who are married to non-indigenous Fijian males are not entitled to be registered in the *Vola ni Kawa Bula*. The discrimination against Fijian women in this respect is clear.

A recent Court of Appeal ruled that, in rare exceptions, a legitimate child born of a indigenous mother and a non-indigenous father could be registered in the *Vola ni Kawa Bula*, provided, among other things, that the relatives in the clan in which the person was claiming membership were willing to accept the person as one of their own that the person had performed the necessary customs to the satisfaction of the mother's clan and the Native Lands Commission; and that there was a general consensus by members of the *mataqali* for his or her entry to be a member of the clan.

This decision is not necessarily an advancement of women's rights in Fiji, as registration remains dependent on arbitrary acceptance.

D. The application of customary law

Article 100 of the Constitution recognizes customary law except where the law is repugnant to or against the general principles of humanity. Although it is not clear what the consequences are for women, if the customary laws are patriarchal, then women may be disadvantaged by the application of customary law. This means that if the customary laws are based on equality and are just and fair to women, and the law is applied by just and fair judicial officers, the customary laws will not be discriminatory to women. If, however, the customary laws are based on patriarchal principles, then the laws will be applied to women in a discriminatory way.

A disturbing feature about customary law is that the decision of the Fiji Native Land Commission as to whether or not a matter is one of custom or tradition is considered final and may not be challenged in a court of law. This means that if the Native Land Commission makes a decision with regard to women that is discriminatory on the ground that it is customary law, they may not challenge the decision in a formal court of law.

In Fiji, the formal courts have accepted the traditional custom of *bulubulu* in rape and domestic violence cases. This has resulted in convicted criminals escaping imprisonment. The *bulubulu* in a rape case is an act of apology by the rapist's family for the behaviour of the rapist in harming the person and dishonouring the family. The underlying rationale is to preserve good relations between the families despite the wrong done and ought to be without prejudice to criminal punishment because the *bulubulu* is not meant to excuse conduct.

If the *bulubulu* is accepted, which in most cases it is, because of the enormous pressure on the woman, this is offered in court by the rapist to reduce his sentence. In Fiji, with few notable exceptions, most rapists who perform *bulubulu* are excused from further punishment. The Courts therefore misinterpret the custom to the advantage of the rapist.

On the other hand, the *bulubulu* in an affiliation case is both an act of apology and recognition that the child has been fathered by a male member of the family making the approach. In this case, it is consistent with the requirement for some proof of paternity. However, the Courts have mostly not accepted the *bulubulu* as proof of paternity arguing that if the alleged father does not participate in the ritual, he cannot be taken to have approved of the *bulubulu*.

Commentators suggest that the *bulubulu* is being used improperly against women when, historically, it could not be used to escape punishment in rape cases.

It is the intention of the Government of Fiji to set up traditional Fijian courts to administer customary law. As in other Pacific island countries, minor criminal matters and the area of personal law will fall within the jurisdiction of these custom courts. According to the proposed legislation, the custom courts will only affect indigenous men and women. Persons from other races will continue to have access to the mainstream Westminster-style legal system. Women's organizations have expressed grave fears for indigenous women as women's experiences of custom, village, island or traditional courts in the Pacific islands have, in the main, worked against them. Fiji women who do not support the introduction of the custom courts maintain that the proposed Fijian courts system will reinforce traditional attitudes and values which will further oppress women.

1. Affirmative action provisions

The 1990 Constitution has specific provisions to make laws for the benefit of disadvantaged groups who have traditionally been denied access to resources or who lag behind in education and development. Under Article 18 it is possible for the legislature to pass affirmative action laws and for the government to create policies and implement them to advance the status of women. The government has only used this provision to date to create and implement policies in favour of indigenous Fijians. It has been suggested that it is difficult to see how Article 18 could be used to advance women's status given the racially discriminatory provisions of the Constitution, which have negative implications for all women who are non-Fijian. Despite this perspective, it is desirable that Article 18 remain, otherwise laws or policies which would aim to advance any disadvantaged group including women would be illegal.

Under Article 18 it would be possible to reserve parliamentary representation or establish quotas for women.

E. Nationality law

1. Discrimination against foreign husbands of Fiji women

The Constitution and Citizenship Act, Cap 87 makes foreign women married to Fiji men eligible to apply for Fiji citizenship by registration upon marriage. In addition to eligibility for citizenship, foreign women married to Fiji men may live in Fiji without the need to apply for a residency visa. They are exempted from the requirements of a visa under the Immigration Act. In effect, foreign women married to Fiji men acquire a "permanent residency" visa which enables them to stay in Fiji. If such foreign wives wish to work, they need to apply for a work permit but this is generally granted.

In comparison, foreign men married to Fiji women are not eligible to apply for Fiji citizenship, by registration. Further, they may not reside in Fiji without a tourist visa or a work permit. They are treated in the same way as ordinary expatriate or tourists applying for residency and work permits in Fiji. They do not get "permanent residency" visas. To satisfy the requirements for a work permit, foreign husbands must obtain work and prove that they are not competing with a Fiji citizen for work. If foreign husbands wish to apply for citizenship they may acquire citizenship by naturalization. This means that they must, like all other ordinary applicants, fulfil the requirements of Article 17 of the Constitution, which includes residence in Fiji for five years either continuously or in total aggregate.

The overall effect of such provisions is that Fiji women have to leave Fiji because their husbands cannot remain. Women who marry foreigners have to thus surrender their birthright and leave Fiji. The provisions of the Constitution and legislation therefore discriminate against Fiji women in terms of eligibility for citizenship as well as residency.

2. Discrimination against women's children born overseas

If a woman married to a foreign male gives birth to her child whilst overseas, her child is not eligible to apply for automatic citizenship rights in Fiji.

Article 25 of the Fiji Constitution states that,

"A person born outside of Fiji after the 6th of October 1987 shall become a citizen of Fiji at the date of his birth if at the time of his birth his father is a citizen of Fiji".

A child born overseas to a foreign woman married to a Fiji man is given full rights of Fijian citizenship.

However, an exception in the Constitution allows a child born overseas to a Fiji mother married to a foreign father to claim citizenship through a grandparent who is a Fijian citizen. This exception does not, however, remove the discriminatory aspects of this law against Fiji women.

An illegitimate child born overseas to a Fiji female citizen is automatically entitled to Fijian citizenship.

F. Family law

For the most part, the family law legislation is written in a gender-neutral style. It is discriminatory towards women in its interpretation, procedure, practice and effect. Patriarchal judicial attitudes influence decision-making and reinforce women's subordinate legal status in relation to men. Family law, more significantly, has a negative impact on women because of their subordinate economic, political and cultural status.

The common law on domicile requires women to live where their husbands wish them to live. Women are required to prove fault in order to obtain maintenance. The grounds upon which maintenance may be obtained include proving fault of habitual drunkenness; adultery; desertion; persistent cruelty; failure to maintain; or if the husband is suffering from a venereal disease and has knowingly passed this disease onto his wife; or if he has forced his wife into prostitution. The married woman may then apply to the court for custody of her children and for maintenance for herself and children. Proof of fault requires independent evidence.

Women encounter great difficulty in proving fault, especially cruelty and adultery, which are among the most common grounds. Cruelty towards a wife is regarded as part of a wife's lot and is difficult to prove. Wife beating is sanctioned by most communities. Only physical cruelty is a ground for separation and maintenance. Mental cruelty is generally ruled by the courts to be an insufficient ground unless it is accompanied by physical cruelty. Adultery by husbands is common and is regarded as forgivable. Adultery by women, however, appears to be rarely forgivable. Witnesses and family members are often unwilling to attend court and women face great pressure from family members to remain in marriages irrespective of the circumstances. The discriminatory aspects of these laws are thus intensified due to social mores and pressures.

These fault-based grounds are exhaustive and if there is conflict in a married relationship which falls outside these grounds, maintenance will not be granted to the wife if she leaves her husband. Given that women have very little access to paid employment, a maintenance law based on fault seriously disadvantages women and children.

If a wife commits adultery, even if it occurs after an initial separation through the husband's fault, she is not entitled to claim maintenance for herself. Adultery automatically disentitles a wife to maintenance even if her husband deserted her and left her without means of support. If she was obtaining maintenance, it ceases upon proof of her adultery. A wife's maintenance is therefore granted in exchange for her lifelong fidelity to a man she is no longer living with, even if her husband has remarried or is in a de facto relationship with another woman.

Maintenance awards do not adequately cater for women's needs. They range from between F$5 and F$12 per week per child. Maintenance awards are based on the duplicate principles of the needs of the wife and children and the ability of the husband to pay. Courts seem to give little regard to these axioms and indeed appear to favour affluent men who pay disproportionately small amounts of maintenance in relation to their incomes.

In addition, the Courts have developed a practice not to order more than one third of a defendant father's income in maintenance notwithstanding the twin canons of need and ability of the defendant to pay. Given that women generally secure custody of children and consequently have a greater financial need than defendant fathers, the one-third rule would appear to be inequitable.

De facto wives and children do not have the same rights as legal wives and children. Only legally married women may claim maintenance from their husbands. Natural children, however, may claim maintenance from their fathers if the mother can prove paternity. De facto wives generally have no right to claim matrimonial property under matrimonial laws or pensions; nor do they have the right to seek the protection of a non-molestation order.

The laws of paternity require "corroboration" of the complainant's evidence before a magistrate can find that the defendant is the "putative" father of an illegitimate child. Corroboration is evidence of an independent nature which tends to prove the truth of the complainant's evidence. Corroboration is extremely arduous to find and women encounter great difficulty in proving paternity.

The main consideration in assessing fitness for custody of children in family law legislation is, theoretically, "the best interests of the child". A legally married mother does not have an automatic right to custody. Both parents have an equal right to secure custody save that when the children are of "tender age" (under five years) there is a presumption in favour of mothers.

Although it is specifically legislated that the welfare principle is the paramount consideration in custody matters, there has been a primary focus, not upon women's mothering role, but rather upon aspects of women's sexual behaviour. This troublesome focus has successfully mitigated against women being awarded custody.

Divorce law is based on proving fault and thus fortifies a cultural milieu dedicated to entrenching the institution of marriage and deterring women from obtaining divorce, no matter the circumstances. The grounds upon which divorce may be obtained are, for the most part, gender-neutral and include adultery; wilful or constructive desertion; wilful and persistent refusal to consummate the marriage; habitual and persistent cruelty; a finding of guilt in a court of law of rape of another person, or bestiality with an animal or sodomy; habitual drunkardness or intoxication from drugs for more than two years; unsoundness of mind, or insanity; separation for more than five years and presumption of death.

The law covering the distribution of matrimonial property between husband and wife following divorce is not based on the principle that women have an automatic legal right to share in this, even if the wife wins custody of the children. Property laws are based on the principle of "justice and equity", but in practice gender discriminatory values affect the interpretation of "equity" and the assessment of relative contributions to family income and welfare which is used to determine it. The inequity inherent in the equity principle comes from the fact that the courts attribute a value only to the "economic" monetary contributions made by both partners to the family income and exclude the "value" of the domestic, unpaid labour performed by women. The ultimate effect of this can be (and is often) that dependent wives who have spent years raising children, looking after the home and producing food from subsistence agriculture and fishing are disqualified from any claim to a share of property once the marriage ends and, despite having custody of the children, are left homeless. The only exception to this would be the rare case of a woman's name being on the title to the property alongside her husband's or where a wife is earning and is able to secure her interest with a caveat and thereafter prove economic contribution.

A combination of laws, court procedures, precedents and judicially imposed practices together make for a system that operates against women, especially poor and working class women. It is clear that women of the privileged classes of the major ethnic groups are protected from the more dire consequences of the system, at least as long as they remain married or are economically independent. Many women have also made great advances in commerce, industry and government. However, these women make up only a small percentage of the total population of women.

Discriminatory constitutional provisions, other discriminatory laws, practices and structures which give women different treatment from men reinforce and entrench the disadvantages that women currently face. Thus, discriminatory laws act in concert with other economic, political and social forces causing overall severe disadvantage to Fiji women.

G. Economic rights and employment law

1. Economic status

Women's economic status in terms of their lack of earning power and access to income contributes to their secondary status in the community. In Fiji, the average participation rates in paid labour, according to the 1986 census were 23 per cent for females and 85 per cent for males. The census also reported that only 23 per cent of women were economically active, compared to 85 per cent of men, but if this included homemaking, then 84 per cent of women are economically active compared to 85 per cent of men. The Household Economic Activities Survey data indicated that female participation had increased to 55 per cent for females by 1989-1990 but the increase is not noted in official estimates. Some of the increase in women's participation in paid employment is through their increased participation in the garment industry.[14]

In 1989-1990, 10 per cent of heads of household were women. In total, the number of paid workers and self-employed persons in 1992 was 171,572. Of these 29 per cent were women.[15] The majority of Fiji women are concentrated in unpaid labour, mainly domestic, and subsistence agriculture and fishing. Indigenous Fijian and ethnic Indo-Fijian women have approximately similar numbers in the paid workforce (11,532 and 11,007 respectively) but a smaller percentage of Indo-Fijian women are economically active relative to the number of Indo-Fijians in the population.[16] In 1989, the average salary was F$8,055 per year. The average salary of females in formal labour has been estimated at 88 per cent of the male average.

---

[14] Ibid.

[15] Ibid.

[16] Atu Emberson-Bain with C. Slatter, *Labouring under the Law*, Fiji Women's Rights Movement, 1995, p. 11.

Employment in the Civil Service accounts for about one third of formal sector employment and women make up 44 per cent of this. Women are concentrated in the Ministries of Health and Education, are in the lower rungs of the employment ladder and are rarely found in administrative and managerial positions. Only 1 per cent of employed women are in this category and only 8 per cent of all administrative and managerial positions are held by women. Females comprise only 8 per cent of upper positions, 20 per cent of middle positions and 48 per cent of lower positions. Within this category, Indo-Fijian females are more disadvantaged than Fijian females.[17]

Women are under-represented in formal sector agriculture but over-represented in professional/technical and clerical occupations. There was also a marked increase of women in the manufacturing industry from 1985 to 1989.

The informal sector covers economic activity in households but also in manufacturing. In comparison to the formal sector, women participate in larger numbers in this sector of employment (36 per cent). The average income of paid workers in subsistence agriculture, forestry and fishing is F$335 per month and women earn 64 per cent of the average male income.[18]

Some women are obtaining access to income by becoming self-employed. These women are not accounted for in the statistics but they are making significant contributions to the family income and to the economy.

Overall, women earn lower wages than men, they have poorer work conditions than men, they are confined mainly to junior positions, have little access to promotional opportunities, are engaged primarily in non-unionized labour and are concentrated in community, public or personal service whether unskilled (domestic work, office cleaning, waitressing), skilled (clerical work, stenographers) or professional (nursing, teaching). Women also have a higher rate of unemployment (15 per cent) than men (5 per cent). Most areas of women's work are unorganized. There are only a small number of trade unions in the "women's" industries. Large numbers of women report sexual harassment.[19]

In all areas of employment, Fijian males are more advantaged than Fijian women, Indo-Fijian men and women and others; Indo-Fijian men are more advantaged than Indo-Fijian women and others; and Fijian women are more advantaged than Indo-Fijian women and others. Overall, rural Fijians and Indo-Fijians are less advantaged economically than urban dwellers in all categories.

Taken together, all these factors mean that the majority of Fiji women are engaged in work that does not earn them money. Therefore, only a minority of women are economically independent. The majority of women are dependent on male incomes whether it be their husband's money or their male relatives' money or on receiving maintenance.

---

[17] *Women of Fiji: A Statistical Gender Profile*, p. 18.

[18] Ibid.

[19] Project report, Fiji Women's Rights Movement, 1995.

This prevents women from having access to wealth, land and independent economic power without reference to men. Women's secondary economic status thus worsens the discrimination that they face in other areas. It is clear then that having access to adequately paid work is more problematic for women than discriminatory laws which affect their status in the workplace.

2. Employment law

The law reflects conservative views about women's proper status as wives, mothers and teachers and the expected domestication of women. This dominant ideology is carried over into the paid workforce affecting women's low wages, their access to employment, the restricted categories of work available to them, their dominance in the lower echelons of formal employment, the lack of legislation protecting their work and their vulnerability within labour.

It is important to note that, although the laws affecting women's work have a significant role to play in determining women's status, women's situation in labour is more significantly shaped by broader non-legal political, social and economic forces. The law merely reinforces women's poor position within labour.[20]

Wages paid to male workers in all categories are based on the notion that men are natural heads of household responsible for their immediate families and other dependants. The payment of lower discriminatory wages to women is based on assumptions that women's participation in the wage market is discretionary and is a means of obtaining pocket money.

Particular categories of workers are excluded from the advantages of maternity leave under the Employment Act, Cap.92: casual workers, those who have been employed for less than five months and domestic workers. Under the same legislation, other workers need only be employed for three months to enjoy annual leave benefits. There is no legal provision to excuse pregnant women from heavy labour, to protect them from exposure to harmful substances, nor from working excessively long hours.[21]

Fiji female civil servants have the right to a total of 84 days fully paid maternity leave under the Fiji Government Leave Regulations (1972, Section 18) for the first three pregnancies. After the first three children, women may get annual leave up to 84 days but without pay. This leave is discretionary.

For women working in the private sector, Section 74 of the Employment Act covers their rights during pregnancy and maternity. Women may not be dismissed if they cannot return to work after taking 42 days maternity leave. Whilst they are on maternity leave they are entitled to F$5 per day of leave. They may stay away from work for a further three months after their normal maternity leave terminates as long as they have a medical reason approved by a doctor.

---

[20] Emberson-Bain, op. cit., pp.1-4.

[21] Ibid., p. 11.

Unlike other Pacific island countries but like Solomon Islands, Fiji law does not permit women two one-hour nursing breaks a day. Women also have no protection from dismissal if they take more than the extra two weeks maternity leave allowed by law with a doctor's certificate even if they are certified medically unfit to resume work. Women may not, furthermore, choose to take their 84 days leave in one block (after birth as most women would prefer) but are obliged to take this leave in two blocks, 42 days before and after birth. In practice, it is possible to take this leave in one block but it is the sole discretion of the employer.[22] Another disturbing feature is that women who exercise their option to work during their pre-confinement and post-confinement period may not be compensated for forfeiting their leave unlike other workers who are entitled to leave pay if they forfeit their leave (Section 75, Employment Act).[23]

Sexual harassment is common, especially in industries like the garment industry, which is dominated by women and non-unionized, as illustrated in 1989 when garment workers protested over compulsory body searches by security guards.[24] Women do not enjoy the same opportunities as men in the labour force and are usually employed in low-paying, low-skilled jobs which have male supervisors, like the garment industry. This inevitably allows sexual harassment to flourish. As there are few laws protecting women workers and women have fewer financial options, most women have to continue working in a hostile environment.

There is no specific legislation against sexual harassment in the workplace or elsewhere. Currently, complaints are handled by union officials or organizations like the Fiji Women's Rights Movement or the Women's Crisis Centre which try to negotiate on behalf of the woman, particularly if she wishes to remain employed.

Many categories of women's work are not explicitly legislated for e.g. domestic work, the garment industry and other industries dominated by women. Current interpretation of employment legislation by government ministries holds that domestic workers (including cooks, house servants, child nurses, gardeners and washerwomen) are not covered by the Employment Act.[25] Thus, such women workers have no statutory benefits such as paid annual and maternity leave, nor do they have the right to seek worker's compensation in case of injury.

H. Women in the criminal process

Trafficking in women and girls is not an issue for Fiji women. Neither is violence against women in the situation of war or internal displacement.

---

[22] Ibid.

[23] Ibid., p. 12.

[24] *The Fiji Times*, 27 January 1989.

[25] Emberson-Bain, op. cit., p. 11.

1. Criminal assault against women in the home
(domestic violence)

In over 95 per cent of domestic assaults in the Pacific region, the husband is the aggressor.[26] Yet it is common in the Pacific for those in power to claim that women are as much to blame as men, that women provoke or cause the beatings. The latest argument in the equality debate is that women are beating men just as often. What these attitudes fail to understand is that the vast majority of assaults in the home are committed by men against women. Further, a slap on the wrist or even to the face is not quite the same thing as a kick in the head or a punch to the stomach.[27]

The reasons for which men beat women also seem trivial in comparison to why women beat men. Women hit their male partners in desperation, frustration, usually in self-defence and usually only once.[28] On the other hand, men hit their partners from reasons ranging from a meal not being ready, for dressing a certain way, to "answering back".

According to the Fiji Women's Crisis Centre, domestic violence occurs in one out of every four or five marriages. In 1983, due to pressure from the Women's Crisis Centre, separate statistics for criminal assault in the home were collected. In the Southern Division alone (covering Suva) 183 domestic assaults on wives were reported to the Suva Police. Reports suggest that only 10 per cent of women report abuse.

Table 1. Criminal assault on wives reported between 1988 and 1992

1988	1989	1990	1991	1992
123	175	212	245	248

Source: Fiji Women's Crisis Centre.

Of those who reported criminal assault, only 10 per cent reported these assaults to the police.[29] The number of women seeking assistance for the first time at the Fiji Women's Crisis Centre in Suva has increased tenfold since its inception in 1984. In 1993, 1,300 women sought the assistance of the Centre. Of these, 43 per cent were seeking assistance due to criminal assault in the home.[30]

Police statistics for 1993 show that there were 348 domestic disputes involving husband and wife reported to the police station. Of these, 72 per cent involved assault, occasioning actual bodily harm, and almost all of the remainder involved common assault, throwing objects or acting with intent to cause grievous harm. Husband and wife disputes accounted for 295 (84.7 per cent) of all domestics disputes reported to the police.[31]

---

[26] *Pacific Island Month*, October 1992.

[27] *MS Magazine*, Sept.–Oct. 1994.

[28] *Confronting Violence: A Manual for Commonwealth Action*, Commonwealth Secretariat, 1992, p. 7.

[29] C. Carter, *Fiji Women's Crisis Centre Booklet*, NSW Tafe Commission, 1992.

[30] *Women of Fiji, A Statistical Gender Profile*.

[31] Ibid.

Of the 500 divorce cases filed by the Office of the Public Legal Advisor (Legal Aid, Social Welfare) in 1988, approximately 20 per cent of these were filed on the basis of persistent cruelty. More than 50 per cent of these cases involved varying degrees of domestic violence although divorce was not filed on this ground as persistent cruelty is very difficult to prove. Most women wait out the lengthy five-year separation period which does not require proving fault on the part of the husband before filing for divorce.[32]

Pacific women enjoy little protection under the law in domestic assault cases. The paucity of the legislation and the laxity in enforcement of the law intensifies social and cultural mores which coerce women to remain in violent marriages, no matter the consequences. Violence, or the threat of violence, is the means by which women are socially controlled in all major cultures under the pretence that it is culturally acceptable to beat women.

The law on domestic violence is informed by such societal mores as the notion that marriage is a private matter between husband and wife, that women subconsciously enjoy being beaten, that alcohol causes wife abuse, that women deserve being beaten and that if women were really being hurt they would leave their husbands. Domestic violence occurs with impunity because it is a crime committed against women who are usually physically and economically powerless and who usually have no alternative but to remain in violent marriages irrespective of the consequences.

Characteristics of the legislation, legal conventions and judicial and police attitudes are significant in determining the position of women in the law as victims of domestic assault. Currently, their position has the following features: domestic assault is unrecognized as a separate crime against women; police and law enforcement officials are unsympathetic and in the main do not encourage legal solutions; it is the chore of the victim to lay charges; it is difficult to enforce a non-molestation order; there is a consistent focus on reconciliation notwithstanding the circumstances; magistrates rarely if ever impose custodial sentences to reflect the seriousness of the crime; there is a tendency for Courts to punish with bind-over orders despite domestic violence being a recidivist crime and the *bulubulu* is accepted by the Courts in lieu of punishment of the offender.

The police is the only agency of the state which is virtually everywhere, even on remote islands in the Pacific which have no major urban centres. It is also the only agency which is available on a 24-hour basis and has enormous resources and power at its disposal to actually do something about responding to cries for help by women in the home.

The legislation requires the police to prevent crime and to arrest those who commit crimes. The current police response to criminal assault against women in the home throughout the Pacific almost without exception is that these matters are "domestic" and women have no place reporting an assault to the police in the first place or proceeding to prosecution. This is an unofficial practice of the police influenced by cultural attitudes.

---

[32] P.I. Jalal, *The Urban Woman, Victim of a Changing Social Environment in Environment and Pacific Women: From the Globe to the Village*, in R. Leautuailevao and J. Taeiwa, *Fiji Association of Graduates, Proceedings of the Biennial Convention*, University of the South Pacific, 1988.

Police practice in the Pacific is that upon arrival at the scene of the crime they attempt to calm the parties down, to mediate or negotiate a settlement or reconciliation and then to refer the parties onto a village elder or a religious minister if no settlement is obtained. Arrest rarely occurs even where the woman is begging that the abuser be arrested. Experience shows that the man is usually arrested, not when he continues to hit his wife in front of the police, but when he gets into a fight with the police.

The police place greater value on the privacy of the family and on the marital rights of the husband than on the rights of the woman. Most police who are influenced by their own cultural attitudes and beliefs believe that the woman probably provoked the violence anyway. If there is the slightest chance that the matter will not end up being prosecuted or if prosecuted will not result in a conviction the police quickly lose interest. Their view is reinforced by women who make complaints and when pressured by their husbands or families, withdraw criminal charges.

In late 1995, the Fiji police force initiated an innovative "no drop" policy in relation to criminal assault against women. The policy dictates that the police are obliged to criminally charge all offenders no matter the circumstances. Despite the "no drop" policy, the Courts are still excusing offenders without punishment[33] at the trial level.

In Fiji, if the offenders and victims are indigenous Fijians, the Court will accept in lieu of punishment that a *bulubulu* was offered to the wife's family and accepted. The victim herself has little say in the outcome as enormous pressure is placed on her to accept the "apology". By giving offenders suspended sentences or accepting the *bulubulu* so that offenders do not serve a custodial sentence, the law effectively gives implicit authority to wife-beaters to continue beating their wives. This means that the Court sanctions violence against women.

Another feature of the law in Fiji on criminal assault against women in the home is the consistent focus on reconciliation or settlement no matter how serious the violence. There are numerous cases in Fiji of the enormous pressure put on women to become reconciled with their husbands.

Women are bullied and harassed by the magistrate, prosecutor and the defence counsel (lawyer representing the abuser husband) in court to withdraw all criminal charges for all sorts of reasons.

In criminal charges it is the responsibility of the person making the accusation of a criminal offence, the complainant, to press charges and to push for the accused to be prosecuted. It is therefore the wife's responsibility to make a statement about the assault and to initiate the prosecution. This takes great effort and persistence. The prosecution cannot proceed without the complainant's cooperation. In another words she is the primary accuser. The onus is on her to proceed with charges against an offending husband in all Pacific island countries. This is a procedural matter and part of the normal criminal process.

---

[33] *The Daily Post*, 16 January 1996.

Punishment of domestic assault offenders is taken very lightly and it is rare that an offender is actually imprisoned. The maximum length of imprisonment possible in the Magistrate's Court or other courts of first instance ranges from between three months to five years imprisonment.

The available civil remedies or solutions for women in the Pacific currently are fairly limited. The criminal options and the limitations of this remedy have already been discussed previously. Civil remedies require the woman to do something about the violence herself in a civil suit. In a criminal case the state is in charge of the matter. The civil options are limited to:

- Simple separation or separation and taking out a maintenance and/or custody case or divorce
- Applying for an injunction or non-molestation order
- Suing for damages or compensation for trespass to the person

2. Sexual assault

Crimes of a sexual nature against women and children (mainly girls) are generally not reported. Nevertheless, between 250 and 300 cases are reported to the police every year. About one third of these are rape or attempted rape cases, a quarter are indecent assault and a quarter are defilement of a girl under 16 years of age.

Rape is a serious felony and is punishable by life imprisonment. According to the legislation, the only matter to be proved is whether or not the woman consented. Rape occurs upon penetration. If the woman did not consent, then it is rape. The common law, however, has built in a number of requirements based on certain notions about women's roles and sexual behaviour. Among these are the notions that rape is always accompanied by violence and therefore there should always be visible injuries; that women say "no" when they mean "yes"; that most women precipitate and enjoy being raped; that women often cry rape for reasons of revenge, pregnancy or if they are caught having sex with somebody inappropriate; that women provoke rape by their behaviour and dress; that rape is sex and not violence and that rape with a foreign object is not rape. These beliefs find expression in the way that women are treated by law enforcement agencies, in the length of sentences meted out to rapists, in various legal rules and procedures and in the way that rape trials are conducted in court. The following is illustrative of the genre;

> "I find from the record that this is an exceptional case. I can understand the offence of rape for which perhaps a sentence of 18 months imprisonment is adequate. But I find that the accused has brutally assaulted the woman with a cassava (an indigenous root crop). It is an inhuman and dastardly act which deserves severe punishment. I can understand the accused having the human temptation because according to him at the time his wife was living away from him. But I cannot understand how a normal human being could have done such a thing as indecently assaulting a woman with a cassava."[34]

---

[34] Jesuratnam J., *The Fiji Times*, 25 July 1988.

The comments reveal commonplace judicial attitudes, namely, that a sentence of 18 months for rape is a sufficient penalty, that an act of rape with a penis is less violent and not as criminal as rape with a foreign object, and that rape (a non-consensual criminal act) is a reasonable alternative to sex (a consensual non-criminal act).

Marital rape is not a crime even where the parties are separated. Rape is technically not a reconcilable offence as only minor crimes can be reconciled. However, in practice, many Courts treat rape and indecent assault as reconcilable. It is currently the only serious crime capable of being reconciled.

The uncorroborated evidence rule in the law of rape also provides an example of how the form of law, particularly in its procedural rules, defines the relationship between the parties before the dispute presents itself and is thus weighted against female victims. The warning by the judge to the jury that it must be cautious about convicting the accused rapist on the uncorroborated evidence of the complainant has the effect of making the complainant's evidence immediately suspect and less credible. The evidence of women and children in sexual complaints is considered innately unreliable.

The underlying assumptions of female sexuality that inform the law are socially constructed and reproduced in the law. The ideas informing the law structure the definition of rape around an opposition of chastity and unchastity, so that a rapist is only punished if he rapes a chaste woman. The Courts appear to be sympathetic to a victim if her behaviour is comparable with appropriate female sexual behaviour. If a woman walks the streets, or goes to a nightclub, she then becomes disentitled to the protection of the law. If a woman acts too "freely", for example, drinking in pubs or associating with various men, her consent is either assumed or irrelevant. A woman's implied bad character is therefore admitted into evidence.

Questioning of the victim's past sexual experience during a rape trial is permissible, and evidence of her moral character may be admitted as evidence against her. There are numerous accounts of acquittals and reductions in sentences based on the victim's sexual and moral behaviour. A woman's past sexual experience is rendered as evidence against her to show that she has consented to the act of sex, the implication being that if a woman is not a virgin it is quite likely that she would have consented to sex with the accused. In one case the High Court gave two rapists suspended sentences because the girl lived "a loose form of existence".[35]

It is instructive that the law allows a woman's past sexual experience (non-criminal behaviour) to be brought into court as evidence against her, but it does not allow the rapist's past (criminal) history as evidence against him until after the conviction has been obtained, if it is obtained. Thus, if the rapist has committed rape previously, this evidence cannot be admissible until after conviction, if it is obtained. This procedural rule favours men over women and is discriminatory.

Rape sentences indicate that offences against property are more likely to attract custodial and lengthier sentences than rape. An illustration of this occurred when a man who raped a housewife was sentenced to 18 months imprisonment. On the same day, two youths

---

[35] *The Fiji Times*, 23 February 1988.

who stole goods to the value of F$445 were sentenced to two years imprisonment.[36] Penalties range from probation to six years. Eighteen-month to two-year sentences are more common, with suspended sentences being increasingly awarded.

In 1988, in response to intense lobbying by the Fiji Women's Rights Movement, the Chief Justice issued a new "Rape Sentencing Guideline".[37] The guidelines clearly stated that the starting point for rape sentencing was five years in a contested case and more, depending on the aggravated circumstances of the case. Furthermore, a sentence of less than two years should never be imposed under any circumstances and a two-year sentence was only acceptable when the accused plead guilty.

In 1990, new guidelines were circulated,[38] taking back much of the 1988 guidelines. It was stated that the 1988 guidelines might have been put too high and as a result might place an undesirable fetter on the discretion of magistrates when sentencing for rape. It stated that there might be occasions when a non-custodial sentence might be appropriate. More recently, in 1994, the Court of Appeal created a new precedent by stating that the starting point for rape should be seven years imprisonment.[39] There has been some positive response to this precedent but the majority of Magistrates Courts still award inadequate sentences.

3. Prostitution

Prostitution is illegal. The legislation is gender-neutral and applies to the following persons who are associated with prostitution: the prostitute who is caught loitering or soliciting in public places for the purposes of prostitution; the male "pimp" or female "madam" who organizes the prostitute and who earns money from the prostitute; any male person who assists a prostitute to ply her trade; and the person who keeps a brothel or who allows prostitution to be carried out on his or her premises.[40] Penalties range from fines to imprisonment.

The most notable aspect of the legislation on prostitution is that the client or consort (mainly male) who uses the services of the prostitute is not committing a criminal offence. Despite the gender-neutrality of the legislation since mainly women are prostitutes and men are clients and there is very little organized prostitution in Fiji affecting pimps and madams, the laws making prostitution illegal affect mainly women, poor women. Therefore the law is indirectly discriminatory towards women.

---

[36] *The Fiji Times*, 30 December 1987.

[37] Circular Memorandum No. 1 of 1988, Judicial Department.

[38] Circular Memorandum No. 1 of 1990, Judicial Department.

[39] *Mohammed Kasim v The State*, Criminal Appeal No. 21 of 1993.

[40] Penal Code, Cap. 17 (ss. 166, 167 and 168).

4. Abortion

Whether or not abortion should be legal or illegal is an extremely controversial subject in the Pacific Islands as everywhere. This is so even though abortion using traditional methods such as local herbs, the insertion of foreign bodies into the womb, ritual massage and bathing are common throughout the Pacific.[41] There are loosely two sides in the abortion debate.

Even pro-women activists are hotly divided on the issue. Pacific women's NGOs have tended to stay away from the issue for political reasons because they do not want to cause divisions amongst their membership. They prefer to concentrate on issues which they argue are more immediately pressing and which will not cause divisions.

Induced abortion is illegal in all Pacific island countries. Although abortion is a criminal offence, there are a number of exceptions to the general rule.

Legal abortion is available to women in Fiji if can be proved that the abortion is necessary to save the mother's life. That is, it is a defence to a charge of illegal abortion for the doctor to say that the abortion was done to save the mother's life. The "saving of a mother's life" is subject to a number of different interpretations.

When an abortion is done to preserve or save the mental or physical health of the mother, this is termed a "therapeutic" abortion. It may not result in a criminal prosecution or it will be a good defence to a charge of illegal abortion.

The legislation in Fiji permits abortion where it is done to preserve the mother's life.[42] In the Fiji case of *R v Emberson*,[43] the Court ruled that if a doctor did an abortion in good faith for honest and sincere reasons because he honestly believed that the mother's physical and mental health was in danger, it was a legal abortion. That is, it was one that fell within the exceptions to the law against abortion and the doctor had a good defence to the charge of conducting an illegal abortion.

The State v Indar Wati, Fiji[44]

The Facts:

A 46-year-old woman was charged with procuring an abortion for a young woman under Section 172 of the Fiji Penal Code. The defendant did the abortion with a "cassava" stick. She inserted the cassava stick inside the young woman's womb and three days later the young woman developed labour pains. She later delivered the foetus at a medical clinic. The young woman testified that she was poor and that if she

---

[41] M. Pulea, *The Family, Law and Population in the Pacific Islands*, University of the South Pacific, Institute of Pacific Studies, 1986, p. 102.

[42] Penal Code Cap. 17 s. 234.

[43] Criminal Appeal No. 16 of 1976.

[44] *The Fiji Times*, 16 December 1993.

had been forced to have the baby, she would have been shunned by her family and would never have been able to marry. She said the stigma of being an unmarried Indo-Fijian mother would have been "very nasty". The defendant was not paid for the abortion but did it as an act of friendship because of the young woman's desperate circumstances.

The decision:

The Court gave the defendant a suspended sentence.

The Court appeared to take into consideration the fact that the young woman who had become pregnant would otherwise have suffered the social stigma of being an unmarried mother in a community where pregnancy outside marriage was not accepted.

Although it is not legislated, abortion seems to be available fairly simply in Fiji in cases where a pregnancy arises out of rape or incest. This is regarded by hospital authorities as abortion for reasons of the mother's mental health.

At recent Fiji Annual Medical Conference,[45] it was reported that 62 per cent of doctors responding to a survey were against abortion but 54 per cent of these said that they might change their minds depending on individual cases. The doctors who agreed with legalizing abortion (38 per cent) said that they would carry out such an operation up to the twelfth week of pregnancy.

Abortion has always been practised in Pacific cultures. The adoption of Western laws and Christianity attempted to put a stop to it. It continues to be practised quietly even where the law makes it illegal. This is really a law that is against poor women because rich women will always be able to pay for an abortion to be done by competent doctors secretly and can, if they wish, go overseas to countries where safe abortion is legally available. If it is illegal, poor women have to resort to "back street" abortions which may be unsafe. This law puts the lives of poor women in danger.

5. Infanticide

The killing of a child by its mother is considered murder unless it can be proved that the killing was due to post-natal or after-birth mental and psychological depression. If a Court accepts that the mother killed her child due to post-natal depression the criminal charges may be reduced from murder to infanticide. Generally a mother who takes the life of her child is charged with murder but the charges are reduced to manslaughter and she then may be found guilty of infanticide.

The woman who is being prosecuted for killing her child must be able to prove through the expert opinion of a psychiatrist that she did not really understand the consequences of her act at the time the offence was committed.

---

45   *The Fiji Times*, 18 May 1993.

If the judge is sympathetic she may get a very short sentence. Unfortunately, that sympathy depends on the personal views of the judge and there have been some instances where woman who should have been found guilty of infanticide were found guilty of murder and sentenced to long terms of imprisonment. If the Court has a genuine understanding of the issues associated with infanticide the woman may get a short sentence and sometimes even a suspended sentence might be imposed.

This means that if a woman kills her child who is under the age of 12 months, after birth or while she is breastfeeding, due to some form of post-natal depression, the Court may find her guilty of the lesser crime of manslaughter, in this instance termed infanticide, instead of murder. However the maximum penalty for manslaughter is the same as that for murder, that of life imprisonment.[46]

Sentences of women who kill their children range from imprisonment to suspended sentences. The women are found guilty of a range of offences from murder to infanticide. If a woman is found guilty of infanticide, rather than murder, she is treated as if she had committed manslaughter.

In Fiji, a pregnant squatter woman who killed her baby daughter by dropping her into a neighbour's well after suffering many months of criminal assault in the home was found guilty of manslaughter, rather than murder. The woman was originally charged with murder but the charges were reduced to manslaughter. The woman lived in conditions of great poverty in a squatter settlement. She was imprisoned for nine months.[47]

The State v Mala Wati[48]

This woman was given a two- year suspended sentence for causing the death of her five-month-old baby. The Court noted that the woman, a victim of criminal assault in the home, and a solo mother of seven children, was

> "...bathing her baby...inside her squatter dwelling. The baby was hungry. The accused due to her financial predicament, found it difficult to feed her baby regularly. The baby was crying and writhing in hunger. The accused had no food to feed the baby. In anger she lost control of herself and strangled her child until he was dead".

In this case the High Court accepted that the woman had committed the act because of

- Post-partum depression
- The distressing circumstances of her poverty

The Court then gave the woman a suspended prison sentence upon her plea of guilty to infanticide.

---

[46] ss. 198-201, Penal Code, Cap. 17.

[47] *The Fiji Times*, 23 October 1993.

[48] *The Fiji Times*, 27 October 1993.

The issue of infanticide is both complex and controversial. The attitudes of the Courts vary from outright condemnation which views the act as murder to leniency which views the act as infanticide which is caused by post-natal depression. The condemnation has much to do with the fact that the law cannot reconcile mothers who kill their children with the belief in women's traditional roles as child-bearers and child-carers. Infanticide challenges society's belief that women have "natural" roles as primary care-givers and that the "maternal instinct" is inherent in all women.

The main causes of both abortion and infanticide are rooted in the difficult conditions of women's existence. Both events, which are criminal offences, occur because women in the Pacific have very little control over their own fertility and access to contraception and because of the social and economic conditions under which they live. The law is also influenced by predominant Christian religious beliefs and social attitudes towards mothers and children. The law's treatment of offenders varies in the Pacific but generally women who commit infanticide are treated more leniently than women who commit abortion.

There appears to be little logic in laws which view abortion with such severity, yet when a woman gives birth to a child that she obviously does not want and thereafter kills it the law's attitude can be one of sympathy. It seems that the law and society are more sympathetic to a woman who kills her living child than one who aborts her unborn foetus.

I. Conclusion

Feminist lawyers and feminists engaged with the law are torn between two opposing viewpoints. The two viewpoints are these:

- The law is inherently flawed against women. The patriarchal basis of the law is so deep that it can never be changed to accommodate a woman's perspective. The law will always resist feminist change. It is therefore pointless to even engage with the system or participate in it. By doing this, feminist lawyers are making the system legitimate, they are upholding the very system that they believe to be so flawed.

- The law is flawed, it does discriminate against women directly and indirectly and does legitimize inequality. However, it would be impossible to replace it with something else in the short term. Society is stuck with an established legal system. Feminist lawyers have to work within it despite its shortcomings to help individual interests. Nevertheless, they must never forget the shortcomings of the system for women, nor their part in making it legitimate (and therefore acceptable).

Thus, feminist lawyers are torn between upholding the law and working against it. Most realize that it is a practical impossibility to do otherwise than to work within it to change it from inside, yet most believe that the law is internally flawed.

What does feminism combined with this understanding teach women lawyers and activists about the law?

- Not to assume that just because something is part of the law that it is inherently just or fair for all or for women;

- Not to assume that because a law is apparently gender-neutral it affects women and men in the same way. The question must always be asked, if a decision is made a certain way what will the effect of that decision be on that woman?

- Not to assume that the law is neutral and impartial. The law serves the interests of the most powerful members of any given community, that is, those who have money and power. Those who control the major institutions of society, the economy, the judiciary, the legislature and the executive (government);

- That it is not sufficient to change the laws. This is ultimately useless unless there is a broader transformation of the economic structures and class relationships that affect women;

- That sex discrimination and affirmative action legislation try to solve particular features of gender inequality. Whether or not legislation makes a difference in the long term depends on other forces that are beyond the scope of the legislation itself. Social and economic inequalities cannot be removed by legislation. However legislation has a major role to play in the overall achievement of an equal society;

- A legislative strategy may address some expressions of gender inequality and attempt to attack some of the foundations of sexism which are part and parcel of most institutions of society. However, it is not possible to legislate allegiance to non-sexist attitudes. In the final analysis, amendments to the law promoting the equality of women can and will only be enforced by those who have the necessary commitment. Changes to other institutions of society will only occur when there is an overall breakdown of patriarchy.

The inherent contradictions that are faced by feminist lawyers and activists have been elegantly put:

"The feminist lawyer must recognize that the struggle within the legal system using the processes of the law has built-in-contradictions which I have mentioned. The feminist lawyer must recognize the realities that I have mentioned – that while feminist litigation has its uses in present times, the ultimate goal of feminism is to destroy patriarchal structures (the legal system included) and with this in mind, she must never be co-opted into the system. The non-lawyer activists have a significant role in this process – not only to prevent the co-option that I speak of – but to wage, in arenas other than the legal system, the struggle of women that will influence the struggle within the legal system – and eventually redefine the realities, the terms, the rules of the women's struggle in the legal realm."[49]

---

[49] Eleanor C. Condo, *Gender and Access to Justice: The Challenges Ahead in Gender and Access to Justice: A Report of the Regional Training Programme*, Asia Pacific Forum on Women, Law and Development, 1992.

Third World feminist lawyers and activists do recognize and accept that if there is a feminist outlook on the law it can be an instrument that can serve women. They accept that it has shortcomings and that the law has an oppressive function but that it also has the potential to have an empowering function, to help women gain some independence and freedoms. At worst it helps individual women, especially poor women, gain some rights. At best teaching women information about the law and how to use the law brings with it a growing consciousness that there are powerful interests at stake behind the law. The law is still a legitimate site upon which women need to wage a struggle. Women in the third world cannot face the luxury of ignoring it.

Knowledge of the law and understanding patriarchy through it brings women to feminism. Knowledge of the law's treatment of women builds an anger at injustice, and through that anger is born a feminist consciousness. For this reason alone a challenge to the legal system cannot be ignored.

In the end, if the law is a servant of patriarchy, then to challenge the law means that there is an indirect attack on the master. It may not be possible to use the master's tools to bring down the master's house but it may be possible to use the master's tools to make cracks in the walls of patriarchy.

V. INDIA

PROMOTING WOMEN'S RIGHTS AS HUMAN RIGHTS*

A. Introduction

The concept of human rights, premised upon the principle of equality, liberty and justice, has several inherent tensions: the fact of biological differences necessitates a reinterpretation of the principle of equality, and asymmetrical gender relations in society imply that in gender-related crimes, justice to one party is likely to mean injustice to the other. Furthermore, in a world which defines "human rights" as "men's rights", women's rights are predictably sidelined. Thus, in most countries including India, laws and rights essentially serve to protect social and familial structures rather than women as individuals who are institutionally forced into a subordinate gender role and identity.

Seen against this background, the issues of women's rights and protective legislation for women in India are but a culturally specific variation of the universal phenomenon of women's oppression institutionalized in the patriarchal social structure. Crimes against women perpetuate this subordination built into the social-economic structures and value system against which women are helpless, either because they have internalized the value system and are rendered incapable of protest, or because they lack the sympathetic support structure so essential for a viable protest. Efforts, both real and ostensible, have been made for decades to redress the situation through legal and judicial means, without achieving gender justice which remains elusive as long as the deeply social structure and value system remain unchanged. Thus, the task of protecting women's rights, in India and elsewhere, is rendered difficult by the multiple hurdles: sometimes adequate laws are lacking; when adequate laws exist, complaints of offenses against women are often not registered by the police; when such complaints are registered, the cases often do not come up for trial; when the cases are tried, the lawyers and judges share an anti-woman bias which nullifies the original intent of the laws.

Additionally, the legal situation in India is fairly complex in view of the country's legal history under British colonial rule, its multi-religious population and its federal character (with 26 states and seven union territories constituting the Union of India).

After about a century and a half of British imperial rule, India became independent on 15 August 1947, and became republic on 26 January 1950, when the Constitution of India came into effect. The principles of liberty, equality, fraternity and justice underpin the entire Constitution; yet large-scale inequality continues to exist between genders (Poonacha 1995: 82-85), as also among socio-economic strata.

---

* By Meera Kosambi, Research Centre for Women's Studies, SNDT Women's University, Bombay, India.

The population of India (846 million at the census of 1991) is multi-religious, and is governed by two sets of laws: a uniform criminal law and religion-specific civil laws. The British Government of India codified criminal law in 1860 in the Indian Penal Code which was made uniformly applicable to all Indians. However, because of the British policy of non-interference in civil and religious matters of Indians, a uniform civil code was not introduced in India. Each religious community was allowed to observe its own religious law which was separately codified by the British government; however, in a few cases, the Government did enact legislation pertaining to social customs.

The same system of two sets of laws exists today. The Indian Penal Code was made applicable in independent India, but no uniform civil code was compiled. The majority religious community, the Hindus (83 per cent of the total population of India in 1981), are governed by the Hindu Code Bill, and the religious minorities of Muslims (11 per cent), Christians (2.5 per cent) and other smaller religious communities such as the Parsis, Jews, etc. are governed by their own personal laws. In recent years there has been a growing demand for a uniform civil code from progressive thinkers and activists, and drafts for such a code have been prepared. However, the obstacles are many: no religious community is willing to allow a change or "interference" in its personal laws, while the religious minorities fear that the laws of the majority community would be imposed on them. Feminist lawyers have pointed out that such imposition is not intended or even desirable, because the existing laws of every religious community have an in-built discrimination against women, so that an entirely new set of laws will have to be prepared.

A further complication is that some legislation results in central Acts which are applicable throughout the country, while sometimes certain states in the Union introduce laws with only state-wide applicability, thus introducing a diversity of civil and criminal law.

The issues of women's rights in India, under both criminal and civil law, as well as issues of violence against them are based on the near-universal patriarchal premises of male supremacy, female subservience and the view that women are primarily meant to function as wives and mothers (Kosambi 1993). Concomitant with these is the obsession with women's chastity, their seclusion from the male gaze and relegation to the "domestic sphere", as well as the dichotomy between the "good" women who are wife-mothers restricted to the home and worthy of protection, and the "bad" women who step into the "public sphere" and invite "well-deserved" trouble upon themselves. These patriarchal norms form the implicit, and sometimes even explicit, premise of law in India. Coupled with these is the woman's low status within the family and her lack of control over economic resources.

In the case of Hindus, such a general perspective is endorsed by religion, custom and economic structures. The traditional extended Hindu family operates on the system of patrilineal inheritance and male coparcenary of common ancestral property (both immovable and movable) which cannot be divided. In other words, the ancestral property is held by all the males born in the family as coparcenaries; daughters cannot claim a share in the ancestral property in view of the norm of universal and early marriage combined with patrilocal residence after marriage. A daughter is therefore compensated by a portion called "woman's wealth" which consists of money, jewellery, etc. (which is, however, usually much less than the share enjoyed by her brothers) and over which she has complete control, in principle. However, given the patriarchal family structure, the concept of "woman's wealth" exists only in name in spite of nominal legal protection, it has gradually been transformed into "dowry" which becomes a precondition for marriage and which passes into the hands of her husband or his family.

Second, a result of the patrilocal and patrilineal systems is that a woman is regarded by her parents as an unwanted burden and as one who will go to another's house after marriage; at the same time, she is regarded as an "outsider" in her marital family and has a low status until she becomes a mother, especially a mother of sons. The son preference among Hindus is based on the fact that only sons can perform important rituals for the parents and ancestors. This is reinforced by economic considerations such as the responsibility of sons to look after their old parents.

As a corollary, a woman can access power within the family only through her son and is dependent on him in her widowed old age; she therefore tends to be very possessive of him and tries to prevent bonding between him and his wife which would lead to her being neglected/abandoned by her son. The "mother-in-law" syndrome, responsible for the routine harassment/torture of the daughter-in-law, has its origins in this patriarchal structure.

Third, because a woman's usefulness to the family is viewed in terms of her wife-mother role, a widow is considered to be an unwanted burden. In earlier times, a widow suffered a physical death when she was cremated along with her dead husband; when this custom of widow immolation, or "sati", was prohibited by British law in 1829, the widow suffered a civil death. In 1856 a British law legitimized the remarriage of upper caste Hindu widows (which was prohibited by religious law). Today, the treatment of widows has improved considerably, although there is a resurgence of widow immolation in one part of India.

Although this is a predominantly Hindu variation of patriarchy, it also underpins many customs of the non-Hindu communities in India which share the same cultural ethos. Thus, this overall perspective explains the discrimination against women in the Indian society, which is reflected also in law.

The most telling evidence of the general neglect of women in India is the female deficit in the total population, which is contrary to the universal demographic rule of a female surplus. Not only is the sex ratio (number of females per 1,000 males) in India low, but it has been steadily declining throughout the twentieth century, as shown by the decennial census (table 1).

Table 1. Variation of sex ratio (females per 1,000 males)
in India, 1901-1991

Year	Females per 1,000 males			Year	Females per 1,000 males		
	Total	Rural	Urban		Total	Rural	Urban
1901	972	979	910	1951	946	965	960
1911	964	975	872	1961	941	963	845
1921	955	970	846	1971	930	949	858
1931	950	966	838	1981	934	951	879
1941	945	965	831	1991	927	938	894

Source: Census of India, 1991.

B. Women and the law

1. Nationality law

The Citizenship Act of 1955, with later amendments, provides for acquisition of Indian citizenship by birth (e.g. for a person born in India on or after 26 January 1950), by descent (e.g. for a person born outside India of a father who was an Indian citizen at the time), by registration (e.g. for a person ordinarily resident in India or a person married to an Indian citizen), and by naturalization. There is no discrimination on grounds of sex, religion, etc.

However, the provisions regarding acquisition and termination of citizenship are based on the principle of private international law that nationality and domicile of a minor are ordinarily determined by those of his/her father. Thus, in a case where the mother, an Indian citizen, has the right of preferential custody over her minor children, the children still acquire the nationality of their father if he is not an Indian citizen (Manohar and Chitaley 1989: 330).

The state imposition of nationality on women, irrespective of their own stated wishes, occurred at the time of the partition of British India into the independent sovereign states of India and Pakistan in 1947. The triumph of Independence was marred by large-scale religious violence and a mass exodus of people (estimated at 8 million) across the newly created "national" borders separating India from West Pakistan (now Pakistan) and East Pakistan (now Bangladesh). At this time, citizenship was constituted on the basis of the religion of the displaced person before the time of Partition.

During the Partition, women faced multiple dangers: they were assaulted and/or killed by the "enemy", or even by their own men, or killed themselves, for fear of or after being "dishonoured". Many women were abducted and detained, and thus separated from their families who crossed the border and went over to the "other country". Of these displaced women, many succeeded in ultimately forming a stable marriage relationship with their abductors, and settled down to a peaceful life. However, both Indian and Pakistani governments launched a "recovery operation" to retrieve their own women and restore them to their "legitimate" families. All displaced women and their children were classified as "abducted persons". Of these, Muslim women were classified as Pakistani citizens and sent to Pakistan, while Hindu and Sikh women were classified as Indian citizens and sent to India. This was usually done against their wishes because they wanted to forget the initial trauma, did not want to be uprooted again, and were unsure of a welcome from their parental families who thought of them with shame. But the patriarchal State conferred on them a citizenship without citizens' rights (Menon and Bhasin 1993).

2. Family law

(a) Marriage

Marriage is early and universal in India. The minimum legal age at marriage had been 21 years for men and 18 years for women since about 1950; however, the mean age at marriage for men and women, respectively, was 22.3 and 17.1 in 1971, and 23.3 and 18.3 in 1981, as shown by the Census of India, 1981. The marital status of the population of India in 1992 is given in table 2.

83

Table 2. Marital distribution of the population of India in percentages, 1992

Age group	Never married		Married		W/D/S[a] (in years)	
	F	M	F	M	F	M
0-14	98.7	99.6	1.3	0.4	0.0	0.0
15-19	69.7	91.2	30.1	8.8	0.2	0.0
20-24	24.3	59.4	74.8	40.2	0.9	0.3
25-29	7.6	26.7	90.3	72.5	2.1	0.8
30-34	2.7	9.2	93.6	89.3	3.8	1.4
35-39	1.2	3.6	92.7	94.4	6.1	2.0
40-44	0.6	1.9	89.5	94.8	9.9	3.3
45-49	0.4	1.4	84.0	93.7	15.7	5.0
50-54	0.3	1.2	75.6	91.5	24.1	7.3
55-59	0.3	1.0	64.4	88.7	35.3	10.2
60+	0.2	0.9	37.5	77.6	62.2	21.5
All Ages	55.3	46.1	44.2	45.7	2.5	8.2

Source: Sample Registration System, Registrar General & Census Commissioner of India, cited in *India Country Report,* 1995, p. 15.

[a] W/D/S = widowed/divorced/separated.

Several parallel systems of consecrating marriages exist in India. Usually marriages are performed according to the religious rules of the community to which the parties belong. For marriages of two persons belonging to different religions, provision is made by the Special Marriage Act of 1954 (which revised and replaced the Special Marriage Act of 1872). This special form of marriage is available to all irrespective of religious faith, on certain conditions such as the age limit (21 for males and 18 for females) (Desai 1981). However, as a consequence of marriage under this Act, a member of an undivided family of the Hindu, Buddhist, Sikh or Jain religion, ceases to be so. Thus, marriage under this Act amounts to automatic separation as far as a share in the coparcenary property is concerned.

Marriage among the Hindus is governed by the Hindu Marriage Act of 1955 and its subsequent amendments which stipulate the minimum age limit (21 for men and 18 for women), the degree of prohibited relationship between the spouses, and the ceremony which indicates that the marriage is valid.

Marriage among the Muslims is governed by religious law which stipulates that any adult (post-pubertal) male of sound mind may enter into a contract of marriage, though persons of unsound mind and minors (pre-pubertal persons) may be validly contracted into marriage by their respective guardians. A regular marriage is one where the proposal by or on behalf of one party and its acceptance by or on behalf of the other party occurs at one and the same meeting, in the presence of adult Muslim witnesses – two males, or one male and two females. If witnesses are not present, the marriage is not void but merely irregular.

A Muslim man is permitted to have up to four wives at the same time, but it is not lawful for a wife to have more than one husband at the same time.

(b) Dissolution of marriage

Under the Special Marriage Act of 1954, a divorce petition can be presented by either husband or wife on the ground that the respondent has committed adultery, has deserted the petitioner for a continuous period of minimum two years immediately preceding the presentation of the petition, is undergoing a sentence of imprisonment for seven years or more, has treated the petitioner with cruelty, has been suffering from a mental disorder or from communicable venereal disease or from leprosy not contracted from the petitioner.

Under the Hindu Marriage Act of 1955, a divorce petition can be filed on any of the above grounds, or the additional ground that the other party has ceased to be a Hindu by conversion to another religion.

The divorce procedure according to Islam gives men a unilateral advantage over women. A Muslim husband of sound mind, who has attained the age of puberty, may divorce his wife whenever he desires, without assigning any cause. All he has to do is to pronounce words addressed to his wife indicating his intention to divorce (*talaq*) her, three times, either on three separate occasions or in a single pronouncement. The pronouncement may be made either by spoken word or by a written document; it may even be made in her absence, but must be conveyed to her. The wife may divorce her husband only if she has such power under an agreement made before or after marriage. Divorce by mutual consent is also possible.

The Christians are governed by the Indian Divorce Act of 1869 which stipulates different criteria for husbands and for wives. A husband may present a petition for divorce on the grounds of the wife's adultery; a wife has to prove adultery coupled with another offence. Thus a wife's petition may be based on the grounds that her husband has changed his religion and gone through a form of marriage with another woman, or has been guilty of: incestuous adultery, or of bigamy with adultery, or of marriage with another woman with adultery, or of rape, sodomy or bestiality, or of adultery coupled with cruelty, or of adultery coupled with desertion.

(c) Maintenance

Section 488 of the Criminal Procedure Code provides for the maintenance of wives and children in order to prevent vagrancy, or at least its consequences, such as prostitution. Its rationale, in the words of the Supreme Court, is as follows:

> It is intended to fulfill a social purpose, to compel a man to perform the moral obligation which he owes to society in respect of his wife and children. By providing a simple, speedy but limited relief, the provision seeks to ensure that the neglected wife and children are not left beggared and destitute on the scrap-heap of society and thereby driven to a life of vagrancy, immorality and crime for their subsistence (Agnes 1995: 213).

However, the amount payable has not been fixed, and usually ranges from a quarter to one fifth of the husband's income, which is far from being adequate. Second, the right to maintenance is difficult to enforce, because the onus of proving the husband's income and of enforcing the order is on the woman. Furthermore, a certain percentage of a man's salary, his dwelling house and provident fund are protected against outside creditors in order to protect the family. In this case, it serves to protect the errant husband from paying maintenance to his divorced/deserted wife and their children. Also, such a woman, if found to be unchaste or having remarried, is not entitled to maintenance.

The Hindu Marriage Act of 1955 pioneered the right of men to claim maintenance from women on an unrealistic assumption of equality, even though it is obvious that men have an economic advantage over women, as shown in table 3 analysing 60 cases of maintenance filed at a family court in Bombay.

Table 3. Analysis of maintenance cases filed at a family court in Bombay

		Women	*Men*
A.	**Employment pattern**		
	Unemployed	30	3
	Employed	30	57
	Total	**60**	**60**
B.	**Type of employment**		
	Domestic work	8	0
	Unskilled job in factory on daily wages	11	0
	Home-based work	8	0
	Self-employed	0	9
	Business	0	10
	Organized sector	3	38
	Total	**30**	**57**

Source: Flavia, Agnes 1995, *Gender, State and the Rhetoric of Law Reform*, (Bombay, Research Centre for Women's Studies, SNDT Women's University), p. 218.

In the case of Muslim women, the problem of getting maintenance is acute and has been further aggravated by recent, regressive legislation which was passed as a politically motivated step to win the (male) Muslim vote. The Dissolution of Muslim Marriages Act of 1939 denies divorced Muslim women the right to claim maintenance or children's custody. The legislature therefore tried, successfully, to bring the Muslim women under the purview of the secular Code of Criminal Procedure, which makes provision for maintenance in Section 125.

However, the situation was reversed in a landmark judgement and new legislation in 1986, in the controversial *Shah Bano* case. The lady in question had been married 43 years and had three children when, in 1975, her husband remarried and evicted her from the house. After paying a small amount, Rs 200, as maintenance for two years, he stopped. When she filed a case for maintenance, he promptly divorced her in 1978 and paid Rs 3,000 as "mehr" or amount agreed upon at the time of a Muslim wedding. The Magistrate ordered a monthly payment of Rs 25, which was increased to Rs 179.20 on appeal. But the husband, a lawyer who earned over Rs 5,000 a month, went to the Supreme Court which passed a judgement awarding maintenance but also made anti-Islam observations. This led to a strong protest from conservative Muslims, so that the government backed down and passed a new Act, in spite of protest from progressive Muslims and feminists. The Muslim Women (Protection on Divorce) Act of 1986 ostensibly protects women but in reality protects husbands from not having to pay maintenance (Agnes 1995: 229-260).

(d) Guardianship, custody of children and adoption

Of the ancient legal systems, only the Hindu and Roman law provided for the institution of adoption; Muslim and Christian law did not. Even today in India, only Hindu law recognizes adoption; Muslim law and Christian law do not (Diwan, 1989: v). Hindus give a special importance to sons – to continue the family line, perform rituals for parents and ancestors, look after the parents in old age, etc.

The Hindu Adoption and Maintenance Act of 1956 states that any male Hindu (whether unmarried, married, divorced or widowed) who is of sound mind and is not a minor has the capacity to take a child in adoption. If he has a wife living, her consent (either expressed or implicit) is required unless she has renounced the world, or ceased to be a Hindu or has been declared by a court of law to be of unsound mind. If he has more than one wife living, the consent of all the wives is necessary, except for any of them who is disqualified for any of the above reasons.

A female Hindu can adopt a child only if she is of sound mind, not a minor, and not married – or if married, is divorced or widowed or whose husband has renounced the world or ceased to be a Hindu or has been declared by a court of law to be of unsound mind. Thus a married woman cannot adopt a child; only her husband can. Furthermore, if an unmarried woman, widow or divorcee has an illegitimate child, she cannot adopt a child.

(e) Inheritance and succession

The Hindu Succession Act of 1956 excludes the daughter from coparcenary ownership of ancestral property.

In protest against this discrimination, two states in the Indian Union have extended this right to inheritance to daughters by legislation: Andhra Pradesh in south India about 1992, and Maharashtra in western India in 1994.

The Hindu Succession (Maharashtra Amendment) Act of 1994 has, as its rationale, the provision of equality before law as a fundamental right granted by the Constitution of India as well as the desire to eradicate the dowry system which has resulted from the denial of inheritance to a daughter. The Act gives the daughter the same right as the son in inheriting ancestral coparcenary property.

3. Economic rights

(a) Inheritance and property law

See section 5 above.

(b) Employment law

The proportion of gainfully employed women is low: according to the Census of 1991, only 51.6 per cent of males and 22.3 per cent of females participated in the workforce. Women's unpaid household work remains uncounted in these statistics.

Women's paid employment is largely confined to agriculture or the primary sector comprising cultivators, agricultural labourers, livestock and forestry, etc., 81.2 per cent of working women as against 63.5 per cent of working men, as shown by the Census of 1991. A more disturbing finding of *Shramshakti,* the Report of the National Commission for Self-Employed Women and Women in the Informal Sector (1988), was that one third of the households were supported solely by women, and in another third, women contributed over 50 per cent of the family earnings. Also, 94 per cent of all women worked in the unorganized sector, such as agriculture, etc. where they were unprotected by reasonable working conditions or regular employment (cited in *India Country Report*, 1995: 26).

The Equal Remuneration Act of 1976, amended in 1987, makes it mandatory for an employer to pay equal wages (whether in cash or kind) to male and female workers for "same work or work of similar nature", and prohibits discrimination of women on grounds of sex in matters of recruitment, training, promotion and transfer. Penalty for breach of this Act for an employer or a company is simple imprisonment for up to one month and/or a fine up to Rs 10,000. However, this Act does not apply in certain situations where special treatment is given to women in respect of childbirth, retirement, marriage or death.

(c) Social welfare laws

Women were, in theory at least, given control over their bodies when abortion was legalized in 1971 by the Medical Termination of Pregnancy Act which resulted more from considerations of population control than of women's health. The selective grounds on which pregnancy could be medically terminated included danger to the mother's life, mental anguish (for example, when pregnancy was the result of rape), or "failure of contraceptives", and were liberal enough to be used widely.

Additionally, the Maternity Benefit Act of 1961, with subsequent amendments, provides for certain benefits before and after childbirth. A pregnant woman is entitled to a maximum period of 12 weeks of paid leave (of which not more than six weeks can precede the date of her expected delivery). She is also entitled to a medical bonus if no pre-natal and post-natal care is provided by her employer. A pregnant woman cannot be dismissed from work during the period of maternity leave allowed under the Act; penalty for doing so is imprisonment for a term of three months to one year, and a fine of Rs 2,000 to Rs 5,000 for the employer.

Predictably, these very provisions often result in discriminatory treatment against women in terms of recruitment (so as to avoid paying maternity benefits) or in terms of job description so that low-paying jobs can be allocated to women workers.

In a new experiment initiated by the National Commission for Women, "women's courts" have been set up in several places around the country to expedite the settlement of matrimonial disputes which otherwise remain pending before the regular courts for years on end. The process depends on a heavy involvement of non-governmental organizations which already have family counselling centres and which help the judges and lawyers to dispose of the cases expeditiously. The reactions to the scheme from lawyers and from feminists are mixed: some welcome it as a relief measure and others criticize it as an "assembly-line approach". It is still too early to gauge the success of the scheme (Dhillon 1996).

4. Reproductive rights

In the matter of reproductive rights, the situation of Indian women is very complex in that they are rarely in a position to control their own fertility. The number of children (specifically sons) a woman should ideally have is decided by her husband, or more frequently, by his family. The use of contraceptives is similarly determined by him.

Other pressures are exerted by the government through its population control policy which is considerably influenced by international pressures, and which has, over the years, contained an element of coercion. Some years ago, mass sterilization of men was introduced on a large scale, but had adverse political repercussions. Since then, women have been made the chief target of population control measures. Large-scale insertion of contraceptives (intra-uterine devices such as the copper "T", or injectibles such as the controversial Depo Provera), or sterilization operations on women are routinely conducted in government organized "camps". The necessary precautions, such as medical check-ups to establish suitability of the measures, information regarding their side effects or even simple hygiene are usually lacking.

A large number (about 90 per cent) of private hospitals provide maternity care also, and expensive surgical intervention is often advised. Thus, caesarian sections are often performed unnecessarily instead of allowing for a normal delivery, and hysterectomy is performed as a birth control measure (Padmavathi 1996: 40).

The statistics on maternal mortality rates according to the Annual Report of 1983 by the Registrar General & Census Commissioner of India shows that, of all the maternal deaths (100 per cent), almost half (46.1 per cent) occurred in the age group 15 to 24 years, about one third (32.1 per cent) in the age group 25 to 34, about one fifth (18.9 per cent) in the age group 35 to 44, and the rest (2.9 per cent) in the age group 45-54 years.

The higher death rates for women in the reproductive age groups (20 to 34 years) were very pronounced in 1976, though less so in 1991 (see table 4). At both these points in time, this gap is more marked in rural than in urban areas.

Table 4. Age-specific death rates (per 1,000 persons) by sex and rural/urban areas in India, 1976 and 1991[a]

Age group	1976 Rural		1976 Urban		1991 Rural		1991 Urban	
	Male	Female	Male	Female	Male	Female	Male	Female
0-4	54.2	55.9	29.0	30.1	28.1	30.2	15.4	16.6
5-9	4.8	5.4	2.2	3.3	2.8	3.2	1.6	1.5
10-14	2.6	2.6	1.1	1.5	1.5	1.8	1.1	0.9
15-19	2.7	3.1	1.6	2.0	1.9	2.8	1.4	1.4
20-24	3.0	4.4	1.9	3.3	2.7	3.4	1.8	2.1
25-29	3.5	5.0	2.1	3.0	3.1	3.6	2.5	2.3
30-34	4.7	5.1	2.7	3.3	3.5	3.2	2.5	2.1
35-39	4.8	5.3	3.8	3.8	4.3	3.9	4.0	2.9
40-44	10.1	4.9	7.1	6.3	5.8	4.4	4.9	3.3
45-49	12.5	8.1	10.3	7.2	9.3	6.2	8.4	3.8
50-54	20.5	12.7	15.1	11.8	13.5	9.4	12.9	8.1
55-59	29.8	18.7	22.9	16.7	21.3	13.7	20.8	14.3
60-64	52.6	35.0	33.5	23.7	33.1	24.9	32.5	20.5
65-69	59.1	47.3	49.7	40.3	46.8	38.4	42.4	33.9
70+	119.6	85.7	89.7	83.4	98.1	88.9	90.4	78.7

Source: Sample Registration System, Registrar General & Census Commissioner of India.

[a] The death rates for 1991 are estimates and exclude the State of Jammu and Kashmir.

5. Violence against women

Violence, both within the home and outside, remains an all-pervasive fact of women's life in India (Kosambi 1994). Although the phenomenon is widespread throughout the country, its extent is appallingly high in some states in India, as shown by the case of Orissa (table 5).

Table 5. Violence against women in Orissa, 1993-1995

Type of violence	1993	1994	1995
Registered cases of rape	405	422	562
Registered cases of dowry deaths	187	265	314
– Accused charge-sheeted in cases of dowry death	n.a.	n.a.	40
Discovered cases of torture of women	n.a.	n.a.	1,000
– Cases resulting in suicide	n.a.	n.a.	39
– Complaints registered	n.a.	n.a.	742
– Investigation completed	n.a.	n.a.	156

Source: Rajaram Satpathy, 1996. "Crimes against women go unchecked in Orissa", *The Times of India*, 15 July, p. 5.

(a) Domestic violence including wife beating

Until 1983, domestic violence per se, including cruelty, harassment and murder of wives, was not punishable; husbands or in-laws could be charged under the general provisions regarding murder, abetment to suicide, causing hurt and wrongful confinement, under an Act of 1860. These provisions applied equally to strangers, ignoring the specifics of the domestic situation of the woman's emotional and financial dependence on her husband. She therefore found it extremely difficult to prove violence "beyond reasonable doubt" as required by law, or produce witnesses to corroborate her story. Additionally, the beating might not have caused grievous hurt at any one point in time, but its accumulated effect caused grave injury and mental trauma over time. The problem was aggravated because often the police refused to register a wife's complaint against her husband even when it caused grievous hurt, on the premise that a husband had a right to beat his wife and the wife herself was severely censured by the police and by the community at large.

The Criminal Law (Second Amendment) Act was passed in 1983, to amend Act 45 of 1860 in the Indian Penal Code (IPC).

Section 498A of the Indian Penal Code stipulates that the husband or husband's relative/s who subject a woman to cruelty is punishable with imprisonment up to three years and also a fine. In this connection, "cruelty" is defined as conduct which is likely to drive the woman to commit suicide or to cause her grave mental or physical injury or danger to life, limb, or death. This unfortunately excludes the everyday violence experienced by most women. "Cruelty" also includes harassment with the intention to coerce the wife or her relative/s into meeting unlawful demands for property (though the word "dowry" is not used). Since the police still often refuse to register a complaint of domestic violence, allegations of dowry harassment are added on to strengthen the complaint, with the result that the case does not stand legal scrutiny and the husband is acquitted.

Usually, however, the ill-treated wife chooses not to file a complaint in view of her own insecure position because her right to the matrimonial home is not protected by law, or under family or public pressure; or she subsequently withdraws the complaint because the husband makes it a precondition for reconciliation, or because of the intricacies of the legal proceedings if she opts for divorce.

Table 6. Reported cases of domestic violence in Greater Bombay

Year	Murders section 302 IPC[a]	Suicides section 306 IPC section 304 IPC	Harassment section 498A IPC and sections 3,4,5 of DPA[b]
1986	4	38	41
1987	12	45	143
1988	2	56	152
1989	13	103	177
1990	9	72	143

Source: Flavia Agnes, 1995. *Gender, State and the Rhetoric of Law Reform*, (Bombay Research Centre for Women's Studies, SNDT University, RCWS Gender Series, Gender & Law: Book 2), p. 7.

[a] Indian Penal Code 1860.
[b] Dowry Prohibition Act 1961.

(b) Marital rape

Marital rape is not recognized as an offence. Section 375 of IPC which defines rape states that "sexual intercourse by a man with his own wife, the wife not being under 15 years of age, is not rape". If she is below this age, the husband can be punished with simple or rigorous imprisonment of up to two years and/or a fine.

Section 376 states that forced sexual intercourse by a man with his wife during separation does amount to rape but it incurs a lower punishment than ordinary rape: namely, imprisonment of either description for a term up to two years and a fine. The logic for reduced punishment is that such sexual intercourse, although forced, might lead to reconciliation, which is viewed as the most desirable situation.

(c) Dowry and dowry murders

Dowry-related harassment and torture, sometimes leading to murder or suicide, is a peculiarly Indian form of violence, and has been instrumental in activating the women's movement in recent times. A case which sent shock waves through the nation involved 20-year-old Sudha Goela who was married to Laxman Kumar of Delhi in 1980. Following repeated dowry harassment, she was finally set on fire 10 months after her wedding. At the time she herself was eight months pregnant, and the crime was timed so as to prevent her from delivering her child and thus consolidating her position within the family or from demanding maintenance in case of desertion. When the neighbours saw the fire and tried to rescue Sudha who was in flames in the backyard of the house, they found the doors of the house firmly barred. The family fabricated a written "dying declaration" ostensibly made by Sudha, explaining her death as an accident while cooking on an open stove. However, on the basis of the neighbours' testimony, medical evidence and Sudha's own oral dying declaration, the Sessions Court convicted Laxman Kumar. The Delhi High Court acquitted him, but the Supreme Court upheld the original verdict. However, the death sentence was commuted to life imprisonment because during the intervening years, Laxman Kumar had remarried and his second wife was pregnant (Mehta and Dighe 1991: 19).

Legislative attempts to prevent dowry extortion have failed consistently. The Dowry Prohibition Act of 1961, amended in 1984 and 1986, seeks to eradicate the custom of dowry altogether. However, it has proved to be ineffectual because the term "dowry" is defined very narrowly as property given in consideration of marriage and as a condition of the marriage taking place. It excludes presents in the form of cash, ornaments, clothes and other such articles; and equally important, it also excludes such demands made after marriage.

The Act lays down punishment of five years and a fine up to Rs 15,000 or the value of the dowry, whichever is more; but it does not apply to presents given to the bride or the bridegroom. It is possible for the girl's parents, relatives or a social work institute to file a complaint on her behalf; it is a cognizable and non-bailable offence with the burden of proof on the accused. If the woman dies an unnatural death, her property would devolve on her children, or, in the event of her being childless, revert to her parents.

Needless to say, the Act has failed almost totally in protecting women. Section 304 B of IPC deals with dowry deaths. If a woman dies of burns or bodily injury, or even dies under normal circumstances within seven years of her marriage, and if it is shown that soon before her death she was subjected to cruelty by her husband or his relatives in connection with a dowry demand, such a death is called "dowry death" and the husband or his relatives are held guilty of her death. The burden of proof is on the accused and the punishment is a minimum of seven years and a maximum of life imprisonment.

This Act is also ineffectual because it is extremely difficult to prove harassment "beyond reasonable doubt". The seven-year limit is also arbitrary.

(d) Wife murder

The legal provisions applicable in this case are Section 302 of the IPC dealing with murder which is punishable with a death sentence or imprisonment for life and also a fine, and Section 306 of the IPC dealing with abetment to suicide which is punishable with imprisonment of either description for a term up to 10 years and a fine.

(e) Widow immolation or "sati"

The custom of cremating the widow alive on the funeral pyre of her just-deceased husband was prevalent in some parts of India in the early nineteenth century, and the British Government of India enacted legislation to abolish "sati" in 1829 in some major provinces of India, such as Bengal, Bombay and Madras Presidencies. This provision to prevent the commission of "sati" was not incorporated in the Indian Penal Code enacted later, on the understanding that the Sections dealing with murder, suicide and abetment to suicide would be sufficient to deal with the offence (Agnes 1995: 151-173).

The practice of "sati" was presumed to have stopped long ago. However, in 1987 the country was shocked by the reported incident of "sati" involving Roop Kanwar, an 18-year-old college-educated girl, in a village in the state of Rajasthan in northwest India; there was an overwhelming demand for a new legislation on an issue which had been dealt with 160 years earlier (Poonacha 1994). The state immediately passed the Rajasthan Sati (Prevention) Ordinance, which was followed by central legislation known as the Commission of Sati (Prevention) Act of 1988.

Thus, widow immolation is considered to be a special offence, distinct from murder and suicide. The debate surrounding the issue, both in 1829 and in 1987, centred on issues such as freedom of religion and action. However, it has been effectively established that the act of "sati" is not voluntary but the result of emotional and physical coercion; usually the widow is drugged when she is led to the funeral pyre. (Even when such coercion is absent, the widow's willingness to immolate herself, which resulted from the internalization of norms over generations, cannot be said to be "voluntary".) This amounts to her public murder by her marital family which thus succeeds in retaining her dowry/property, and at the same time, gaining "spiritual merit" status in the community, and wealth collected from pilgrims who visit the "sati" commemorative temple erected for the purpose. Thus, in reality, it is a case of calculated murder rather than suicide, although the conservative justification is camouflaged as a human rights issue.

However, the Act of 1988 makes the attempt to commit "sati" punishable with imprisonment for a term up to six months and/or a fine. Abetment, direct or indirect, to the commission of "sati" is punishable with death or life imprisonment and also a fine; the burden of proof rests on the accused. The glorification of "sati" through ceremonies, processions, commemorative temples, etc. is punishable with imprisonment for a term of one to seven years and a fine of Rs 5,000 to 30,000. The District Collector and District Magistrate are empowered to take steps to prevent "sati" in any area where such a likelihood exists. These officers are also empowered to remove "sati" commemorative temples and to confiscate funds or property acquired in connection with "sati". All offences under this Act can be tried only by a special court constituted for the purpose.

(f) Female infanticide

The Female Infanticide Prevention Act of 1870 was made applicable to certain parts of India, especially in the north and north-east where the custom was prevalent; it could be adopted also by any other province.

The Act sought to prevent the murder of female infants by introducing imprisonment for up to six months and/or a fine up to Rs 1,000. In addition, it empowered the District Magistrate to take measures to prevent female infanticide, for example, by maintaining a register of births and deaths, by taking a census of communities suspected of such a practice, by maintaining a special police force or officers to prevent and detect the murder of female infants, and for the regulation and limitation of expenses related to marriage (which was a predominant reason for doing away with girl children). The District Magistrate was also empowered to protect a female child by removing her from the custody of a person who was legally responsible for her maintenance but neglected to do so; he was also empowered to place the child under proper supervision and order the negligent guardian to make a monthly allowance for the maintenance of the child.

The Act was repealed as a whole in 1952 on the assumption that the problem has ceased to exist. The offence of infanticide in general is covered in the IPC by Section 300 (Murder) and Section 302 (Punishment for Murder).

The problem, however, continues to exist in areas which were under observation 100 years ago, specifically the state of Rajasthan, and elsewhere. In 1988 there was a sensational disclosure that a member of the Rajasthan Legislative Assembly belonged to a clan which practised female infanticide: the family had killed 36 female infants during the previous 40 years (Kang 1988). There have been frequent reports that some poverty-ridden districts of the state of Tamil Nadu in the south practise female infanticide routinely in order to avoid exorbitant marriage related expenses (Pandey 1994).

(g) Female foeticide

Selective female foeticide is the latest anti-woman practice which uses the modern technological device of amniocentesis (which diagnoses abnormalities in the foetus) for determining the sex of the foetus, followed by selective abortion of the female foetus. The issue first became public and controversial only when a male foetus was wrongly aborted and the father happened to be an influential government official (Agnes 1995: 174).

Since abortion was legalized and made available under liberal conditions in 1971, the connection between sex determination and selective abortion has been difficult to establish. Also, after government clinics and hospitals were banned from carrying out sex determination tests, women could go to a private clinic for such a test and then to a government hospital for a free abortion.

The issues involved were complex: if a woman has the right to limit the number of children and the right to a safe abortion, it was argued that she had the right to have a child of a particular sex, especially if having too many girls was going to result in marital harassment. Some argued that if girls were subjected to great hardships from birth, it would be humane to get rid of them before birth. The future dowry and marriage expenses have been offered as the chief cause of wanting to avoid having daughters, at any cost: in fact, some unscrupulous private clinics have been known to advertise their services by saying that it was better to spend Rs 500 now (on female foeticide) than spending Rs 50,000 later (on dowry).

In 1984 the Forum Against Sex Determination and Sex Pre-Selection was formed by concerned activist groups. As a result of the campaign, an expert committee was formed by government in 1986; its report was submitted in 1987. In 1988 the Maharashtra Regulation of Use of Pre-Natal Diagnostic Techniques Act was passed in the State of Maharashtra in western India. It stipulated that only clinics and laboratories registered (for genetic counselling, etc.) under the Act, would conduct pre-natal diagnostic tests; that such tests should not be used for indicating the sex of the foetus; that facilities for pre-natal determination of sex should not be advertised; that no pregnant woman or family members should seek such diagnostic procedure for purposes of sex determination. Subsequently a similar but much diluted Act was passed at the all-India level.

(h) Child sexual abuse, including incest

Child sexual abuse is assumed to be widely prevalent in India, as in other countries, but actual data are hard to obtain. The general pattern seems to be the same as in other countries.

In a survey of 348 school and college girls in the city of Bangalore in Karnatake State, it was found that three out of every 20 girls in the survey had experienced serious forms of sexual abuse including rape, and one third of these occurred when they were less than 10 years old. Fifty per cent of the girls had been molested or targeted for sexual overtures as children, and 80 per cent had experienced abuse such as breast squeezing and bottom pinching at an early age. As many as 55 per cent of the abusers were family members – uncles, fathers, brothers, cousins or other close relatives. Several of the girls were unable to cope with their feeling of shame and had attempted to commit suicide. Typically, the girls tried to keep the incident secret because of the shame of losing virginity, the actual trauma, and fear of being maligned (Rai 1994).

Incest remains a taboo subject in India; no official information exists, and a public discussion has started very recently. The laws of rape are applicable to the incestuous sexual abuse of girls, but judges tend to take a relatively lenient view of the matter. An example is the case of 40-year-old man in a squatter settlement in Bombay who raped his eight-year-old daughter in 1985. The Sessions Court gave the man life imprisonment, but when the case came up before the High Court on appeal, the sentence was reduced to 10 years' rigorous imprisonment because of the mitigating circumstances: poverty, close proximity where the family had to sleep huddled up in a small area, sexual deprivation because the man's wife had left him, lack of education, age and the man's "irresistible impulse". Because he was otherwise a "good father" who fed and educated his children, this incestuous rape was considered to be a "momentary lapse" caused by his "pathetic situation" (Times of India, 25 March 1992).

(i) Forced sterilization and abortion

The population control policies of government have led to abortion being made free and relatively easily available. It has also led to the large-scale sterilization of women through tubectomy and the propagation of contraceptive methods such as intra-uterine devices or injectibles without adequate information being given to the women concerned or adequate testing for suitability. (See Section D.)

(j) Forced prostitution and child prostitution

The official view of prostitution is premised upon the patriarchal division of women into "good" and "bad", and the notion that "good" women are wives and mothers who are confined to the domestic sphere and deserve protection from the men outside the family, while the "bad" women are those who enter the public sphere and who are therefore sexually available. Thus, prostitution is tolerated as a necessary evil to satisfy male sexual needs, but the prostitute herself is considered to be an evil woman from whom the rest of the society needs to be protected (Agnes 1995: 127-130).

The Suppression of Immoral Traffic in Women and Girls Act was passed by the government on its own initiative and not in response to activist demands. Basically it penalizes the victim, i.e. the prostitute, rather than protecting her. The Act defines a "prostitute" as a female who offers her body for indiscriminate sexual intercourse, and does so for payment. However, any woman can be labelled a prostitute by the police merely on the strength of her appearance, or the fact of her being out late at night, or any other arbitrary criterion. This encourages police harassment.

This Act was amended by the Immoral Traffic (Prevention) Act of 1988 which stipulated that a prostitute could be punished for soliciting by imprisonment up to six months, or a fine, or both. She can be convicted for any words or gestures used for the purpose of prostitution even from her own house. The police routinely carry out large-scale rounding-up of prostitutes to extract sexual favours and monetary bribes. The sexual exploitation of women through forced prostitution is punishable: living on the earnings of the prostitution of a child or a minor is punishable by imprisonment of seven to 10 years; in the case of similar exploitation of a major the term of imprisonment is two years and a fine up to Rs 1,000. Brothel-keeping is also an offence punishable by imprisonment up to a life term. Male pimps and touts are punishable by imprisonment for seven days to three months. The client escapes punishment totally. The amended Act seeks to prevent abuses by the police by requiring that a search be conducted only with a warrant, or in the company of at least two women police officers. Interrogation of a prostitute can be done only by women police officers, or in the presence of a woman member of a recognized social welfare organization. A medical examination of a prostitute being interrogated is mandatory to determine age or detect injuries caused by sexual abuse. Rehabilitation of rescued prostitutes in suitable protection homes is also mandated, and it is suggested that other gainful employment should be found for them.

(k) Temple prostitution

The system of dedicating very young girls to the service of a Hindu deity, idol or temple stemmed from the belief that the donation of a daughter was a source of spiritual benefit to the parents; but the girls thus dedicated were then forced into prostitution. There is no central legislation to prohibit this practice, but earlier the concerned provinces in British India had banned it, and so have some states in the Indian Union now. Examples are the Bombay Devadasi Protection Act of 1934 and the Bombay Protection (Extension) Act of 1957, the Madras Devadasi (Prevention of Dedication) Act of 1947 and the Andhra Pradesh Devadasi (Prohibition of Dedication) Act of 1988.

All these Acts declare the dedication of a girl as "devadasi" unlawful. They also allow a "devadasi" to freely enter into marriage with any person of the opposite sex, declare such a marriage to be valid and the children of such a marriage to be legitimate.

The above-cited Andhra Pradesh Act of 1988 stipulates that a person who performs, promotes or abets in a dedication ceremony will be punishable with imprisonment of either description for a term of two to three years and a fine of Rs 2,000 to 3,000. In case the "dedicator" is a parent or guardian of the girl/woman, the punishment is higher – his term of imprisonment is to be two to five years, and fine from Rs 3,000 to 5,000. The District Collector or any other revenue officer is constituted as the authority empowered to take steps to prevent such cases.

(l) Rape, sexual harassment and abuse

Sexual harassment is as common in India as in other countries, but currently India has laws related only to rape and not sexual harassment in general. But even this legislation is full of loopholes.

In view of its ever-present threat and the inadequacy of legal protection, rape has been an issue of great concern to women in India. In 1972, a much-publicized rape case galvanized the autonomous women's movement in India. The case involved a 16-year-old tribal girl who had eloped with her lover and who was captured by the police and subsequently raped while in police custody. The Sessions Court acquitted the policemen on the grounds that the victim was "habituated to sexual intercourse" and therefore could not be raped, and further, that she was a liar and had in fact consented to sexual intercourse. The High Court convicted the policemen on the ground that passive or helpless surrender induced by threats or fear could not be construed as consent. However, the Supreme Court reversed the judgement and acquitted the policemen, maintaining that the girl had not struggled with the alleged rapists, and had given her consent to the act. As a result of the nationwide controversy and agitation generated by this case, the old law of 1860 was amended in 1983 (Agnes 1995: 10).

The Criminal Law (Amendment) Act of 1983 defines "rape" as sexual intercourse (i.e. penis penetration) with a woman under any of the following six circumstances: (a) against her will, (b) without her consent, (c) with her consent obtained under threat to herself or a person close to her, (d) with her consent by a man fraudulently posing as her lawful husband, (e) with her consent given in a state of mind (e.g. under the influence of alcohol or drugs) which impedes a clear understanding of the situation, and (f) with or without her consent when she is under 16 years of age. Consent is not necessary when a man has sexual intercourse with his wife who is not a minor.

Punishment for rape is imprisonment for not less than seven years, and may extend to 10 years or for life, and also a fine. Punishment for certain specific categories of rape – custodial rape by the police, rape by public servants or by jail staff or by hospital staff, rape of a pregnant woman or of a woman below 12 years of age, gang rape – is rigorous imprisonment for a term of not less than 10 years and which may be extended to a life term, as well as a fine. In any of these cases, a woman's word as to the absence of her consent is to be accepted.

However, in any case of rape, the court can impose a lower sentence for adequate reasons. Most of the judgements given under this and the previous Act have shown the bias of the judiciary in favour of men. Indulgence towards the "uncontrollable lust" of men and leniency towards youth offenders have been common, while the act of rape is considered primarily not as violence against women but as the violation of one man's sexual property by another man or as a threat to a girl's marital prospects due to loss of virginity (Agnes 1995: 10-85).

Table 7. Disposal of rape cases in greater Bombay, 1985-1989

Description	1985	1986	1987	1988	1989
Registered	101	102	85	108	108
Charge-sheeted	93	96	76	104	100
Convicted	8	1	2	1	1
Acquitted	4	3	1	–	2
Pending trial	81	91	72	102	95

Source: Flavia Agnes, 1995. *Gender, State and the Rhetoric of Law Reform*, (Bombay, Research Centre for Women's Studies, SNDT University, RCWS Gender Series, Gender & Law: Book 2), p. 7.

The emphasis on penis penetration as a criterion for rape means that sexual assault not amounting to rape does not get punished. An army major who roughly fingered the private parts of a seven-and-a-half-month-old baby girl, causing injury, was acquitted by the Sessions Court and the Punjab High Court on the grounds that the act did not amount to the offence of rape, or outraging the modesty of a woman, since the baby was not conscious of ideas of modesty. This last-mentioned view was also expressed by the Chief Justice when the case went to the Supreme Court in appeal.

In order to improve upon the existing legal provisions, the Criminal Injuries to Women and Girls (Compensation) Bill was introduced in the Rajya Sabha (Lower House of Parliament) in 1994 and is yet to be discussed. The Bill seeks to provide for monetary compensation and rehabilitation for women victims of sexual violence and also highlights the fact that most victims of such violence belong to the lower socio-economic strata. Another Bill entitled "Sexual Violence against Women and Children Bill 1993" has been drafted on behalf of the National Commission for Women. This draft Bill broadens the scope of sexual violence to include a range of acts in addition to rape, demands that a woman's past sexual history should not be used in evidence against her, and lays down guidelines for recording of evidence and for medical examination of the victim of sexual violence.

(m) Trafficking in women

See Section 5.J.

(n) Violence against women under war and
conflict situations

Increasingly, rape and sexual assault against women are being used as a means of dishonouring and punishing the "enemy community", especially in cases of religious tension in India. The most dreadful Hindu-Muslim riots in recent times erupted in the aftermath of the demolition of Babur's mosque in December 1992 at Ayodhya in the state of Uttar Pradesh. The worst riots occurred in western India, in the states of Maharashtra and Gujarat, where they served as a convenient excuse for religious violence, mostly by the Hindu majority against the Muslim minority. In terms of sexual violence against women, the worst cases were reported from Surat in Gujarat where women were gang raped in a floodlit open ground and the acts video-filmed by the rioters (Lobo and D'Souza 1993).

(o) Violence against women with disadvantages or
in disadvantaged situation

Women in institutions, such as medical hospitals, prisons, mental asylums, or even in police custody, are vulnerable to sexual assault. Therefore, special provisions have been made in the Rape Law to cover these situations and to stipulate stricter punishment. Predictably, however, these cases rarely get reported and the accused are almost never punished.

A new issue was raised recently, regarding the rights and ostensible measures for state protection of mentally handicapped women. In 1994, mass hysterectomies were conducted on the physically handicapped inmates (aged 13 to 37 years) of a state-run home in Maharashtra, giving rise to a strong protest by feminist activists. The then Chief Minister put a temporary stop to the process, but gradually allowed the procedure to be carried on, provided it was done on a smaller (and less visible) scale. While the doctors defended the procedure as the "internationally accepted medical practice" in dealing with mentally retarded women, the state defended it on grounds that it was well-nigh impossible (due to scarce resources) to maintain the personal hygiene of these women during menstruation, that permission had been granted by their guardians and that this measure would protect the women against unwanted pregnancies resulting from sexual abuse (obviously by the state-appointed staff). The case brought to public notice the complex issues involved in such a situation involving mentally handicapped women (Rao and Pungalia 1994).

(p) Indecent representation of women

Aimed at stopping the degrading depiction of women in the media, the Indecent Representation of Women (Rehabilitation) Act of 1986 applies to advertisements, publications, writings, paintings, etc. and also to films. The offence is punishable with imprisonment up to two years and a fine of up to Rs 2,000.

The pre-existing provisions related to obscenity, as codified in Sections 292, 293 and 294 of the India Penal Code have been ineffectual. Therefore this Act seeks to broaden the scope of "indecent representation" to include the general degradation, humiliation and servility of women. However, this Act has also failed because judges often hold that such servility is the ideal of Indian womanhood.

6. Political rights

Women received the vote at the same time and on the same terms as men, in the general elections in 1923 in British India but the basis of enfranchisement was a series of complicated property and income qualifications which varied from province to province, and within each province. In Madras Presidency, only 10 per cent of the adult male population and about one per cent of the adult female population (who had usually owned little property) formed the electorate in 1923 (Chopra 1993: 14-15).

In 1950 when India became a Republic and adopted a Constitution, universal adult franchise was introduced.

The Government of India has introduced affirmative action for the benefit of the weaker sections of society, by reserving "quotas" for them in certain fields of education, in government jobs, and in political representation. A similar quota for women, to ensure their political representation, was introduced in April 1993, when the Parliament passed the 73rd and 74th Constitutional Amendments reforming the structure of local governments ("Panchayati Raj") on the model of the traditional panchayats or councils of elders (usually composed of five men) which governed the affairs of caste or rural communities. The 73rd Amendment stipulates that 33 per cent of the seats in the rural three-tier local government bodies (the Village Council or gram panchayat, the Council of a Village Group, and the District Council) shall be reserved for women candidates. The 74th Amendment stipulates that 33 per cent of the seats in urban municipalities shall be reserved for women candidates. By April 1994, all the states of India had ratified the two amendments.

The proportion of women representatives in the two Houses of Parliament remains low. During the 11 elections to the Lower House (Lok Sabha) that have been held so far, the percentage of women members has ranged from 3.4 to 7.9 of the total members, ranging from

499 to 545 (Kaushik 1993: 9). Currently, women members form 6.6 per cent of the total of 545 seats. No legislation exists as yet to ensure similar representation for women at the state or national level. The present government has proposed the introduction of legislation giving women 33 per cent reservation in the National Parliament; the modalities of the Act have not been worked out (*Times of India*, 25 July 1996, editorial).

It is difficult to gauge the extent to which the new measures for women's political empowerment have been effective, considering that entrenched social practices are not easily amenable to legal change. There have been cases when women members of village councils have been denied the right to sit on a chair along with the men councillors and made to sit on the floor, underscoring their subordinate position. Again, the village councils are not necessarily in a position to challenge the authority of the caste councils in the village. Very recently, a 26-year-old woman of a low caste was allegedly gang raped by 11 identified persons belonging to her own caste in a village in the state of Uttar Pradesh on the orders of the caste council without the knowledge of the village council. The reason was that the woman, married and a mother of three (possibly ill-treated by her husband), fell in love with a Muslim youth of the same village and eloped with him, thus bringing shame to the whole community. The men of the community felt no compunction in taking the law into their hands and to avenge the "shame" with a criminal offence (Kunwar and Kanth, 1996).

In the face of such a system of values and customs, women's political empowerment seems to be a far-off goal.

REFERENCES

Agnes, Flavia, 1995. *Gender, State and the Rhetoric of Law Reform* (Bombay, Research Centre for Women's Studies, SNDT Women's University, RCWS Gender Series, Gender & Law: Book 2).

Chopra, J.K., 1993. *Women in the Indian Parliament* (New Delhi, Mittal Publications).

Desai, Kumud, *Indian Law of Marriage and Divorce*, 4th ed. (Bombay, N.M. Tripathi Pvt. Led. 1981).

Dhillon, Amrit, 1996. "Women's Courts: Landmark Experiment". *India Today* (30 April), p. 127.

Diwan, Paras, 1989. *Law of Adoption, Minority, Guardianship and Custody* (Allahabad, Wadhwa & Co.).

India Country Report (at the Fourth World Conference on Women, Beijing), 1995. Govt. of India, Dept. of Women & Child Welfare, Ministry of Human Resource Development.

Kang, Bhavdeep, 1988. "Where have all the girls gone?" *Sunday Observer* (4 Sept.).

Kaushik, Susheela., *Women and Panchyati Raj* (New Delhi: Har Anand Publications 1993).

Kosambi, Meera, 1993. Violence Against Women: Reports from India and the Republic of Korea. (Bangkok, UNESCO PROAP).

————, 1994. *Women's Oppression in the Public Gaze* (Bombay: RCWS, SNDT Women's University (RCWS Gender Series, Gender & Violence: Book 1).

Kunwar, D.S., and Kanth, Prityush, 1996. "Panchayat orders U.P. woman to be gang-raped". *Times of India*, 26 July 1996.

Lobo, Lancy and D'Souza, Paul D., 1993. "Images of Violence". *Economic and Political Weekly*, vol. 28, No. 5 (30 Jan.), pp. 152-54.

Manohar, V.R. and Chitaley, W.W., 1989. The AIR Manual: Civil and Criminal,. Vol. 4. 5th ed. (Nagpur, All India Reporter Ltd.).

Mehta, Sudha and Dighe Usha, 1991. "Review of Journals in Regional Languages (Gujarati and Marathi)" in *Women and Violence: A Country Report* ed. by Maithreyi Krishnaraj (Bombay, RCWS, SNDT Women's University) pp. 9-19.

Menon, Ritu and Bhasin, Kamala, 1993. "Recovery, Rupture, Resistance: The Indian State and Abduction of Women during Partition". *Economic and Political Weekly*, vol. 28, No. 17, pp. WS 2-11.

Padmavathi, A., 1996. "Advanced medical technologies: implications on women's health rights". *Legal News and Views*, vol. 10, No. 3, pp. 40-43.

Pandey, Divya, 1994. "Female infanticide: Salem" in *Women's Oppression in the Public Gaze* ed. by Meera Kosambi, 1994 pp. 48-57.

Poonacha, Veena, 1994. "Widow Immolation: Roop Kanwar" in *Women's Oppression in the Public Gaze* ed. by Meera Kosambi, pp. 88-104.

————, 1995 *Gender Within the Human Rights Discourse* (Bombay: RCWS, SNDT Women's University (RCWS Gender Series, Gender & Politics: Book 1).

Rai, Saritha, 1994. "Sexual abuse: shocking facts", *India Today* (31 July), p. 176.

Rao, Nagmani and Pungalia, Sarita, 1994. "Human concern or convenience? Debate on hysterectomies of mentally handicapped" *Economic and Political Weekly*, vol. 29, No. 11 (March 1994), pp. 601-602.

VI. NEPAL*

A. Introduction

Nepal is a multi-ethnic democratic sovereign Hindu Kingdom with a constitutional monarchy. The inhabitants of Nepal are drawn from various religions, such as Buddhism, Islam and Christianity, although the majority of the population are Hindu, a powerful ideological force in Nepal. Hindu cultural values are evident in state governance.

Nepal remains among the 10 poorest countries in the world with a per capita income today of a mere US$ 210. Population growth has overwhelmed the modest gains made in social and economic development. In 1951, Nepal's entire population was less than 9 million. Today, it exceeds 20 million and is growing at a rate of 2.5 per cent every year.

Women account for approximately 51 per cent of the total population. Nepalese women have not made a significant contribution in the development activities of the country due to high illiteracy, poor health, poverty and a traditionally conservative social attitude in favour of men.

Financial resources and opportunities are far from the reach of Nepali women. The average life expectancy of Nepalese women is 53 years compared to 56 years for men. The female literacy rate is 25 per cent, while the male literacy rate is 55 per cent.

As long as women, who constitute more than half of the country's population, are not fully involved in the national development processes, the overall development of the country will not be possible. Hence, programmes and policies must be targeted towards the promotion of women's participation in mainstream development activities, through increasing their involvement in every sector of development, improving their socio-economic, academic, political and legal status, providing productive employment opportunities by increasing their involvement and efficiency through the transfer of appropriate knowledge and skills, creating an appropriate environment so that they are provided with the opportunity to play a substantive role in decision-making from the local level to the national level.

B. International commitments

After the restoration of a multi-party system in Nepal, the government signed the International Covenant on Civil and Political Rights (1966) which recognizes equality before the law and equal protection against discrimination. Nepal also acceded to the Convention on the Elimination of All Forms of Discrimination against Women (1979), without any reservation, in 1991.

---

* By Ms Sapana Pradhan Malla, Advocate.

B. Constitutional guarantees

The Constitution of the Kingdom of Nepal, 1990, provides that there shall be no discrimination against any citizen in the application of laws on the basis of sex. It also empowers the State to make special provisions for women. Besides these rights, the Directive Principles and Policies of the state set guidelines for the state to pursue a policy to promote the female population to participate, to a greater extent, in the task of national development by making special provision for their education, health and employment.

C. Discriminatory legal provisions against women

Nepal has its own idiosyncratic legal system based on Hindu patriarchal ideology which reflects male supremacy. Irrespective of the constitutional guarantees on gender equality, a significant number of laws still exist which are ostensibly discriminatory against women. These laws define women's role as subservient to men: husbands or brothers or sons. However, there is a National Code and eventually there will be only a single set of family laws applicable to all Nepalese citizens.

1. Nationality law

Under the nationality laws a person who is born after the commencement of the Constitution and whose father is a citizen of Nepal at the time of birth of the child shall be a citizen of Nepal by descent.[1]

Every child who is found within the Kingdom of Nepal and whose parents' where-abouts are not known, shall, until the father of the child is traced, be deemed to be a citizen of Nepal by descent.[2]

Women, however, do not have the same right to give such identity to their children by descent as their mother. Women have no right to register the birth of their children. Under the Birth, Death and Personal Incident Registration Act 2033, the right to registration of the child is given to the (male) head of the family, and in his absence to the eldest male member of the family.[3] This means that a woman who carries a human foetus for nine months in her womb has no right to register the name of her own child after birth. These legal provisions manifest the low status of women within the family and in society.

When a Nepalese woman marries a foreigner, she loses her residential right because, after marriage, women, by custom and practice, must live with their husbands. There are no legal provisions for foreign husbands of Nepalese women to obtain Nepalese citizenship on the grounds of marriage. In such cases, even if a Nepalese woman wants to stay in her

---

[1] Article 9(1).

[2] Article 9(2).

[3] Section 4(1).

country of birth, she is deprived as her foreign husband is not even allowed to get a visa to stay in Nepal with his Nepalese wife. The result is that such couples must either live separately and apart or the woman must leave her motherland. Given the acute problems that this situation raises, the Supreme Court has set a legal precedent in the case of *Meera Gurung v. Department of Immigration*[4] that foreign husbands of Nepalese women can stay longer in Nepal as the legal regulations governing foreigners was declared inconsistent with Article 11 of the Constitution which prohibits any discrimination on the basis of sex. Citizenship could not, however, be granted to foreign men.[5]

Judicial interpretation of the nationality laws was considered in *Benjamin Piter v. Ministry of Home.*[6] In this case, although the claim was for a permanent resident visa, the court went further to state that the discrimination created between a male Nepalese citizen and a female Nepalese citizen (under the nationality laws) was contrary to the right of equality guaranteed by Article 11 of the Constitution. Similarly, the same legal provisions were found to be contrary to the various international covenants on human rights which had been ratified by Nepal. Article 11 of the Constitution was considered to be a general provision and those provisions in Part 2 of the Constitution relating to citizenship were considered to be "special provisions". In such cases, it was declared that any agreements made contrary to the "special provisions" could not be held valid and that universal principles (of equality) should be applied.

2. Property laws, inheritance and succession

Discrimination is perceived in the laws pertaining to property. The National Code restricts daughters from sharing in paternal property.[7] A father is not even responsible for providing food and shelter for his daughter.[8] A daughter is entitled to receive a share of the paternal property only if she remains unmarried until the age of 35. However, she must return the paternal property if she gets married,[9] whereas a son's right to paternal property is derived from birth. This provision was challenged in the Supreme Court in the case of *Meera v. Ministry of Law and Justice*[10] which looked into the conditions required to inherit paternal property with a directive order made to the government to bring a Bill within a year to look into the family law. At the same time, the court was also asked to take into consideration the patriarchal society, social structure and a fear of positive discrimination against men.

The laws of succession are discriminatory against women. A daughter cannot inherit her deceased parent's property as long as the deceased is survived by his or her son or the son's son. An unmarried daughter's turn comes only if the deceased has no grandsons.[11]

---

[4] Decision No. 4858, *Nepal Law Journal* 2051 (1994), vol. 2, p. 68.
[5] Article 9(5).
[6] *Nepal Law Journal* 2048 (1992), vol. 11, p. 749.
[7] Section 1, chapter on partition.
[8] Section 10, chapter on partition.
[9] Section 16, chapter on partition.
[10] *Nepal Law Journal* 2052 (1995), col. 6, p. 462.
[11] Section 2, chapter on heirless property.

A deceased woman's exclusive property, if she dies intestate (without a will) devolves to the son who had been living with her or, if she is not survived by a son, the property devolves to her husband. Only if a deceased woman is not survived by her son or husband will her exclusive property go to her unmarried daughter, or if not then to relatives in the following order of succession: to her married daughter, if none, then to her son's son; if none, then to her daughter's son.[12]

Although on marriage a woman is a co-parcener with her husband, she never deals with her share of the family property independently. A wife can legally claim her share of the family property only if she is denied food and shelter by her husband.[13] In other situations, a woman is entitled to receive a share of the property from her husband if she is abandoned by her husband, or if she is treated cruelly or, if her husband marries a second wife.[14] Only in the case of a woman who has completed a minimum of 15 years of married life and who is over 35 years of age, is she eligible to take a share of the family property from her husband.[15]

A woman's right to property is always limited. Laws are formulated in such a way as to ensure that no woman has complete control over her property at any point in time.[16] Her only real property is "daijo", gifts given by her relatives on marriage, and "pewa", gifts given to her husband's relatives or self-acquired property before marriage. However, in law, a woman's "daijo" is limited to 10,000 rupees (equivalent to US$ 200), excluding one set of jewellery, under Section 5(2) of the Social Practice Reform Act 2033BS.

A widow under the age of 30 years is not entitled to take her share and live separately as long as her husband's family provides her with food, shelter, clothing and expenses incurred in pursuing religious activities.[17] A widow's property received from her husband or his family can be forfeited if she is found to be unfaithful to her deceased husband.[18]

On divorce a woman who does not have any earning source of her own is entitled to alimony only for five years or until she remarries, whichever occurs earlier, if the cause for the divorce falls into any one of the following situations:

(i)   Her husband marries a second wife;

- He does not provide her with shelter and food;
- He deserts her for a period of three or more years;
- He causes or tries to cause such acts as may threaten her life;
- He inflicts serious bodily injury to her;
- Finally in the case of her husband becoming impotent.[19]

---

12   Section 5, chapter on women's property.
13   Section 10, chapter on partition.
14   Section 4, chapter on husband/wife rights.
15   Section 10(A), chapter on partition.
16   Section 9, chapter on transactions.
17   Section 12, chapter on partition.
18   Section 6, Chapter on Women's Property.
19   Section 4(a), chapter on husband/wife rights.

The law restricts even those women who have taken their share of property from independently using their property. It requires them to obtain permission from their father if they are unmarried or, from their adult son if married or widowed should they wish to dispose of more than 50 per cent of their immovable property.[20] In the case that a woman receives a share of her husband's property, after the partition, her husband can take a second wife without bringing formal divorce proceedings against the first wife.

If a married woman has physical relations with a man other than her husband she will not have any right to her husband's property. Even for a victim of rape, the law itself states that women shall not be entitled to use the property of the former husband.[21]

From the above provisions, it is obvious that women despite their large contribution in the production of labour, are effectively deprived economic benefits in society. The existing laws prevent women from exercising their equal right to property.

3. Employment policy and labour laws

The state is pursuing a policy of promoting participation of the female population to a greater extent in the area of employment. The international labour standard of equal remuneration for work of the same value is promoted.

(a) New Labour Act and Regulation

After moving towards an economic liberalization policy, Nepal has a new Labour Act 2048 (1992) and Regulation 2050 (1994) which provides the following provisions for women:

(i) Restriction on night work

Women are prohibited from engaging in night work between 6 p.m. and 6 a.m. However, exceptions apply in the following situations:

    a.   The restriction on employment hours for women can be waived after making appropriate arrangements on the basis of mutual agreements;

    b.   Women may be employed by the tourism industry to work at any time after making special arrangements for their security according to the nature of their work;

(ii) Arrangements for babies

    a.   Every establishment employing 50 or more women workers shall arrange a clean and healthy playroom for their babies;

    b.   Breastfeeding breaks shall be granted for women;

---

[20] Section a, chapter on women's property.

[21] Civil Code, chapter on rape.

(iii) Maternity leave

Maternity leave has been increased from 45 to 52 days;

(iv) Equal remuneration for equal work

The principle of equal remuneration for work of equal value is respected;

(v) Restrictions on carrying load

Adult male	55	kg
Adult female	45	kg
Minor male (16-19 years)	25	kg
Minor female (16-18 years)	20	kg
Minor male or female (14-16 years)	15	kg

4. Welfare and education

(a) Welfare policy

Under the directive principles of the state, the state shall make policy in the matter of social security for helpless women: 100 rupee allowances for widows above the age of 60 years will be made by the state as social security for such women.

(b) Education scholarships

An incentive stipend of Rs 25 per month for up to 75,000 primary school age girls from poor families is made to promote education for girls.

5. Family laws

(a) Marriage and divorce

A man can marry another woman in any one of the following circumstances when his first wife is still alive:

- If the wife is incurably insane

- If the wife is crippled and unable to move

- If the wife is blind in both eyes

- If the wife has received her share in property partitioned and is living separately from the husband[22]

- If the wife does not bear any child or the child born does not survive up to the age of 10 years

---

[22] Section 9, chapter on marriage.

Such broad grounds for divorce, however, are not provided to women. For whatever reason that divorce is allowed, the woman must return her share of the property she acquires from her husband's property. A divorced woman is further deprived of any right to her parent's property.

In the case of polygamy committed by the husband, the maximum punishment is one to two months imprisonment and a fine.[23] If a woman marries by lying that she is unmarried, even in the case of widowed women, the marriage is voidable and the woman can be punished by up to one year of imprisonment.[24]

Where a woman commits an offence by engaging in sex with an animal, the maximum punishment is one year imprisonment and up to Rs 1,000 fine. For the same offence where it is committed by a man, the maximum punishment is 6 months imprisonment and up to Rs 500 fine.

In the case of elopement by a married woman, the time limitation on the filing of a case is one year. In the case of bigamy committed by a man, the time limitation on the filing of a case is three months.

(b) Children

(i) Custody

Under the present family laws governing custody of children a second marriage by women will result in the denial of custody to her child or children of the first marriage.

(ii) Adoption

A man is authorized to adopt a child without the necessary consent of his wife. The same does not apply in the case of a woman wishing to adopt a child.

If a family has only one son, such a family is not entitled to allow the adoption of such a son to a third party. The same does not apply in the case of girl children.[25]

6. Criminal laws

Crimes against women or violence against women are prevalent around the world. Such problems are grave in the developing world as a result of the high incidence of illiteracy, poverty and tradition-bound customs and superstitions. A social renaissance is urgently required in this part of the world.

To bring about social reform in these societies is not easy. However, in recognition that it is through legal mechanisms, which control and regulate the socio-legal relationships and which serve as the backbone of reform, necessary policies and reforms for the emancipation of women must be initiated at once.

---

[23] Section 9, chapter on marriage and divorce.

[24] Section 8, chapter on marriage and divorce.

[25] Section 12, chapter on adoption.

(a) Rape

One of the critical issues in Nepal is the existing social violence against women through rape. In the context of the existing laws on rape, the burden of proof lies with the victim. Owing to the social stigma attached to rape and the embarrassment and harassment faced by victims during investigation and prosecution, many cases go unreported. In the open-court hearing procedures, a woman is made to go through the same ordeal many times when she is called to answer and prove her complaint in an open court before male judges and male lawyers. Marital rape does not fall within the definition of rape.

There are different penal provisions for rape depending on the age of the victim. If the rape victim is below the age of 14 years, the offender can be liable for a term of imprisonment for a period between six and 10 years. If the victim is above the age of 14 years, the offender can be liable to a term of imprisonment between three and five years. In all cases, the victim is entitled to receive half of the property belonging to the offender as compensation. The penalties must be stringent in order to deter the commission of such offences. Under Section 10, chapter on rape, the victim is also entitled to use the share of her former husband's property during her life. Once a woman becomes a victim of rape the law assumes her husband to be an ex-husband.

In the case where the victim kills the offender during the attempt of rape or within an hour of the commission of such act, she will be exempted from punishment. However, if she should kill the offender after an hour of such act, she will be liable to punishment of up to a fine not exceeding Rs 5,000 or a term of imprisonment of up to 10 years.

(b) Abortion

Under Nepalese law, abortion is allowed only when performed for the "welfare" of the expectant mother.[26] The "welfare" clause is ill-defined. It does not include the physical or mental health or the life of a woman. It is rather surprising to note that the laws on abortion prescribe a higher degree of penalty for abortion when it is performed with the consent of the mother than an act of abortion committed as an act of intentional revenge or anger by another person. The penalty in the former case is one year's imprisonment for an abortion performed up to the sixth month and one and a half year's imprisonment for pregnancy of more than six months, whereas in the latter case, it is three months imprisonment for a pregnancy up to six months and six months imprisonment for a pregnancy of more than six months.[27]

The Nepalese Medical Council Rules, 1976, state that abortion should be permitted when performed by a registered and trained medical practitioner under the certification of at least two medical doctors that the expectant mother's life is at risk or her physical and mental health is at stake. This notwithstanding, and despite the calls raised by various governmental and non-governmental organizations for amendment of the legal provisions, none have been formulated.

---

[26] Section 28, chapter on homicide.

[27] Sections 31 and 32, chapter on homicide.

The absolute ban on abortion and its criminalization under the law has led many women to untrained hands. This has led to a high rate of maternal mortality and a low health status of women undergoing abortion. As an illegal and criminal act under the law, abortion has further led to a high rate of infanticides committed by the mothers themselves with the result that such women are observed to be imprisoned for a lifetime for such acts. The number of women convicted of infanticide and serving prison terms is very high. It is felt that abortion must be legalized at least in some circumstances. The abortion of a foetus formed as a result of rape or incest, or, with the consent of the couple taking into account the mental and physical health of the expectant mother or, as a counteraction to unwanted pregnancies due to the failure of contraceptives or, if certified by a physician that the pregnancy is likely to yield the birth of a deformed child, should be allowed. A Bill was submitted in the 2025 summer session by the Family Planning Association to legalize abortion. This proposed Bill from the private sector has, however, also included some restrictive clauses such as requiring the consent of a guardian in the case of an unmarried mother, on the consent of the husband in the case of married women, except in the case of rape or incest.

(c) Trafficking of women and forced prostitution

The magnitude of the problems of trafficking women and forced prostitution is enormous. Many factors sustain the system of women trafficking. Poverty and illiteracy are the major and obvious causes, while inadequate legal provisions and the lack of commitment to enforce laws pose as the other major causes to control and eradicate the burning problem of trafficking. The Human Trafficking (Control) Act 2043 BS has been enacted besides the provisions in the National Code. Nevertheless, enforcement of the Act seems to be very weak. Section 4 of the Act prohibits the following activities only:

- Trafficking with any objective

- Trafficking with the purpose of selling women

- Forced prostitution

Prostitution with the consent of the concerned woman has not been defined in the Act. Complaints have to be filed together with the evidence. Most of the time, it is difficult to gather information from the victim. The police have the power to investigate the offence only after getting approval of the court. A victim must face the harassment of police and the public attorney in an open court many times.

The scale of the problem in Nepal was highlighted in recent times by a court order issued in India which returned 128 girls under the age of 20 years, who had been trafficked into India. Ninety per cent of them were HIV-positive. An Indian government source has declared that there are 2 million women trafficked into India, of which 20,000 are believed to be HIV-positive.

(d) Sexual and other harassment

The effect of violence against women in Nepalese society is both negative and serious. Sexual harassment and street teasing keep women in a constant state of exasperation and humiliation, which in turn restricts the freedom of movement of women. No sexual harassment act or domestic violence act exist; there is no separate family law court structure nor even a court in camera to facilitate cases concerning women.

Within the National Code, there is a chapter on the intention to have a physical relationship, which states that if a man touches any part of the body of a woman above 11 years of age who is not his wife with the intention of engaging in physical relations, such a man shall be fined up to Rs 500 or be imprisoned for up to one year.

In other legislative provisions, as Section 2(6) of the Public Crime and Punishment Act, 2027 BS it is provided that no one should maltreat or try to woo a woman in a public place or face a maximum penalty for such offence of a fine up to Rs 10,000 together with compensation which can be claimed from the offender.

Section 8 of the Defamation Act, 2016 BS provides that any person who defames a woman verbally or through gestures or encroaches upon her privacy shall be punished with a term of imprisonment of up to six months and a fine of up to Rs 500.

Apart from the above-mentioned provisions, there is no law on sexual harassment in Nepal. Given the difficulties of evidentiary proof and proceedings conducted in open court format, without the benefit of in camera proceedings together with the fear of stigmatization, no cases under these provisions have been reported.

VII. PHILIPPINES

PROMOTING WOMEN'S HUMAN RIGHTS:
THE EXPERIENCE OF THE PHILIPPINES*

A. Introduction

Women's human rights recently came to the fore in human rights discourse. Although many human rights instruments, including the United Nations Charter have prohibited discrimination on the basis of sex, this has not automatically resulted in the evolution of a distinct women-centred elaboration of human rights concepts. Human rights instruments are supposed to be equally available to both men and women but the invisibility of women's experiences and ideas in the construction of knowledge and in the development of human rights law in general have made this guarantee a very weak one. As women have historically been disadvantaged and silenced, the language of human rights is a potentially liberating and powerful tool for advocacy of women's rights. Women's claims to "rights" looks at the disparities of power according to gender in both the contexts of their private lives and public activities.

Most of the major human rights instruments like the Universal Declaration of Human Rights (1984), the Covenant on Civil and Political Rights (1966) and the Covenant on Socio-Economic and Cultural Rights (1966) prohibit discrimination according to sex. In addition, a number of other international instruments have been especially formulated to address specific issues on women such as the 1949 Convention for the Suppression of the Traffic in Persons and the Exploitation of the Prostitution of Others and previous international agreements on trafficking (1904, 1910, 1921 and 1933), the 1962 Convention on Consent to Marriage, the Minimum Age for Marriage and the Registration of Marriage, the ILO Convention Nos. 100, 111 and 156 on Equal Remuneration for Work of Equal Value and the UNESCO Convention against Discrimination in Education in 1960. The United Nations approval and eventual ratification of the Convention on the Elimination of All Forms of Discrimination Against Women (1979) was a landmark in the history of women's human rights. It consolidated in one document all the previous standards set in previous instruments as well as elaborated on the meaning of gender-based discrimination and called for state accountability to ensure gender equality in all aspects of women's lives. As of 1996, 153 countries had ratified the Convention making it the most widely accepted treaty on women. The convention constitutes a universal and comprehensive document legally binding on all the signatories. However, it

---

* By Aurora Javate de Dios, Member, United Nations Committee on the Elimination of All Forms of Discrimination Against Women (CEDAW); Commissioner, National Commission on the Role of Filipino women; Associate Professor in International Studies and Women's Studies, Miriam College, Philippines.

should also be mentioned that some countries which ratified the Convention placed a number of reservations which tend to lessen the impact of the whole Convention itself. The Women's Convention has currently the biggest number of reservations – 115 among the human rights instruments such that this issue has become a matter of concern to the CEDAW Committee. It should likewise be remembered that the Women's Convention itself was a product of long years of advocacy, moral pressure and hard work on the part of women all over the world. The Women's Convention is also quite distinct from earlier human rights instruments on women on two counts:

- It provides a detailed definition of discrimination against women which includes any difference in treatment by way of distinction, exclusion or restriction on the ground of sex that has the effect or purpose of impairing, nullifying, the recognition, enjoyment or exercise by women irrespective of marital status on the basis of equality with men of their human rights and fundamental freedoms on all spheres of life (Article 1, CEDAW);

- The Convention obligates states to eliminate discrimination both de facto and de jure in all aspects of women's lives such as in marriage, family, nationality, citizenship, health, employment and education through constitutional, legislative, administrative and other measures including the use of temporary special measures aimed at accelerating de facto equality (Article 4, CEDAW).

Despite the impressive gains of women in the field of human rights, there are still major obstacles to women's enjoyment of their legally guaranteed rights. The most serious aspect of this is the issue of violence against women which occurs in the private sphere (domestic violence, incest, marital rape, female infanticide, etc.) as well as in the public sphere (sexual harassment, rape, torture, forced sterilizations or forced abortions) in furtherance of governmental policy, traditional/religious practices such as clitoridectomy, and "sati".

It was the active and organized effort of women's groups in the Vienna Conference on Human Rights that reinvigorated the advocacy for women's human rights centred on the campaign to combat violence against women. The fourth world conference on women held in Beijing in 1995 and its Platform for Action further reaffirmed the commitment of the international community to the full implementation of the human rights of women and of the girl child.

B. The context of women's human rights promotion in the Philippines

The Philippines emerged from the throes of a long period of dictatorship of the Marcos regime through a people's power revolt inspired by a people's movement for freedom and human rights. Tens of thousands of Filipinos were detained, tortured and "salvaged" during the dark days of martial law as their civil liberties and human rights were violated. Thus, the Aquino government was determined to change the culture of violence fostered by the former regime to one that was anchored on the democratic and participative process, including respect for human rights. This augured well for creating the environment for the promotion of human rights in general and of women's human rights in particular.

Another important factor in creating the favourable climate for women's human rights promotion was the strategic role that women's groups and organizations played in the anti-dictatorship movement as well as in catapulting Corazon Aquino into the Presidency. The democratic space that emerged after the ouster of the dictatorship encouraged even more dynamic organizing of numerous women's groups, coalitions and networks which advocated issues on gender equality and women's human rights. As a result of strong lobbying of women's groups, the 1987 Constitution recognizes the role of women in nation-building and ensures the fundamental equality before the law of women and men.

This became the legal and constitutional basis for the pursuance of significant laws and policies relating to women. Although the Philippines ratified the United Nations Convention on the Elimination of All Forms of Discrimination against Women as early as 5 August 1981 and a national machinery for women, the National Commission on the Role of Filipino Women was already there since the late 1970s, women's groups only pursued issues of gender equality and empowerment with more vigour after the 1986 popular revolt. This was quite understandable because during the Marcos regime, it was the First Lady Imelda Marcos who personally led official delegations to the United Nations conferences on women and many women's groups did not want to be associated with her and the regime.

The late 1980s thus marked the highpoint of many initiatives on women including:

- The election of the first woman President who restored democracy in the country

- The formulation of the Philippine Development Plan for Women (1987-1992), a companion document of the medium term plan, the country's socio-economic blueprint for progress and growth. This has now been replaced by the Philippine Plan for Gender Responsive Development (1995-2025)

- The enactment of landmark legislation on Women Republic Act 7192 or the Women in Development and Nation-Building Act

- The institutionalization of gender mainstreaming in the development plans and programmes of government

- In the NGO sector, the mushrooming of women's groups across the country dealing with development issues, political empowerment issues, reproductive rights, violence against women and a host of other issues previously not tackled by political movements

C. The current status of issues and areas of concern for women

While there is no doubt that the government is officially committed to the promotion of women's rights and the elimination of all forms of discrimination, this has to be more concretely implemented in terms of national legislation, administrative policies and programmes that implement legislation and the necessary social and support services to assist women on the road to full empowerment. The following issues and areas of concern need to be assessed as to their adequacy in protecting women's rights.

1. Nationality law

The Philippines follows the *jus sanguinis* rule by which citizenship is conferred by birth to Filipino parents, consistent with the professed state policy of recognition of the fundamental equality of men and women, that Filipino citizenship is vested upon those born of Filipino fathers or mothers. Thus, Filipino citizenship is not denied to children born illegitimately of Filipino mothers and alien fathers.

Another mode of acquiring Filipino citizenship is through naturalization in accordance with procedure set by law. The Commonwealth Act No. 473, Sec. 15 cuts down the procedure of naturalization in cases of an alien woman married to a man who has been naturalized by providing that she becomes a citizen of the Philippines if she may herself be lawfully naturalized. The law also provides that a woman need not prove the qualifications required, she only has to prove that she did not have any of the disqualifications in an administrative proceeding before the Commission on Immigration and Deportation for cancellation of citizenship. Insofar as the law makes it easier for the wife of a naturalized alien to acquire Filipino citizenship, Philippine naturalization policy still remains discriminatory against women.

The Constitution qualifies Commonwealth Act No. 63, Sec. 1, para. 7 regarding the citizenship of Filipino women who marry alien nationals by providing that citizens of the Philippines who marry aliens retain their Filipino citizenship unless by an act or omission they renounce the same. The Commonwealth Act 63 originally provided that a Filipina who married an alien automatically followed the citizenship of her husband if the laws in force in his country conferred his citizenship on her.

2. Family law

The Family Code has been hailed as a progressive law that has significantly modified legal provisions governing family relations in the Civil Code of the Philippines which, in the light of progressively feminist consciousness in the country, were recognized to be discriminatory to women. It took effect in 1988 and since then has had a positive impact on the lives of women. Among the most important provisions of this Code are the following:

- The provision for the annulment of marriage on the ground of psychological incapacity to comply with essential marital obligations (Article 36);

- The equalized age requirement for the capacity to marry of both sexes;

- The elimination of legal obstacles to remarriage afterwards;

- The recognition of foreign marriages (Article 26);

- The expansion of the grounds for legal separation to include inter alia, sexual infidelity (Article 38);

- Joint spousal administration of property and the fixing of domicile (Articles 96, 124 and 152);

- Elimination of the legal obstacles to the contractual capacity of married women;

- Application of the regime of absolute community of the spouses' property in the absence of a marriage settlement providing otherwise. (Article 75)

However, at least two areas in the said Code are still blatantly discriminatory. The first are those provisions which give precedence to the husband's decision in case of disagreement between the spouses regarding administration of property and the exercise of parental authority. The wife is given recourse to the courts for just relief (Articles 96, 124, 211 and 225). The other is Article 46 in which fraud, such as the concealment of pregnancy with another man is one of the reasons for annulment of marriage. However, the code is silent if the man has caused the pregnancy of another who is not his wife.

Under Article 765 of the Civil Code, a husband can revoke a donation in the case of an act of ingratitude of the wife and in Article 238, the husband, if insolvent, may transfer the administration of the conjugal partnership or absolute community to the wife or a third party.

3. Economic rights

A landmark law of far-reaching impact on the economic rights of Filipino women is the Republic Act 7192 also known as the Women in Development and Nation Building Act. The law accords women legal capacity in entering contracts, applying for loans and other credit facilities as well as joining social and cultural clubs. Section 8 of the same law provides for full-time homemakers to avail themselves of social security benefits. The law likewise provides for at least a portion of overseas development aid to be earmarked for projects to benefit rural women.

The law has enabled women to avail themselves of credit facilities in their productive activities. A Grameen Bank Lending programme mostly benefiting rural women reported a successful turnover rate among women borrowers. As of January 1995, the membership to the Grameen type programme totalled 13,528 with about 12,357 members having availed themselves of loans amounting to 31.4 million pesos. Total savings generated by members amounted to 4.2 million pesos.

Women have the opportunity to gain access, control and ownership of land through the land tenure improvement programme of the comprehensive agrarian reform programme. As of 1992, a total of 363,276.65 hectares have been distributed to farmer beneficiaries. These were covered by 270,096 emancipation patents of which only 11.5 per cent went to women. The low percentage of women beneficiaries under the land reform programme can be traced to the low number of female-headed households in the country (14 per cent) and reflects the traditional social norm of giving the prerogative of ownership and inheritance of land to men.

While there is no law prohibiting women's ownership of land, there are no reliable statistics to gauge the extent of women's ownership of real estate. In 1990, the estimate for female headed households was 1.3 million. Of this, 52 per cent reported owning their residential lot; 15 per cent reported owning their residential lots and 26 per cent reported owning agricultural lands.

Other legislation strengthened the economic rights of women:

- Republic Act 6725 strengthening the prohibition of discrimination against women in employment, promotion and training opportunities

- Republic Act 6972 mandating the establishment of day care centres in every barangay

- Republic Act 7322 amending the social security law to increase the maternity benefits of women workers

- Republic Act 7877 anti sexual harassment of 1995 which penalizes acts, behaviour inimical to women in their work places

- Republic Act 7655 which increased the minimum wages of househelpers.

The Labor Code provides night work for women workers at certain designated night time periods depending on whether they work in an industrial, commercial or agricultural setting. Moreover Civil Rule XIV, Sec 12 requires that in the public sector, maternity leave benefits are granted only to married women who are permanently, provisionally or temporarily appointed in the government service. Though these provisions appear to be protective, these policies actually discriminate against women. The night work prohibition has made it easier for women workers to be dismissed and the second makes marriage an entitlement to maternity benefits. Here health benefits do not cover the other health risks of women in their life cycle such as hysterectomy and other reproductive complications.

Despite many enabling laws to empower women economically, many issues still remain among them:

- Gender based discrimination in terms of equal pay for work of equal value, in promotions and hiring practices

- The multiple burden of women workers who continue to bear the burden of housework even as they work full-time in factories and professions

- Lack of economic opportunities and support mechanisms for women in the informal sector

- Occupational segregation in traditional areas of women's work

- The marginalization of women in subcontracting jobs that are exploitative and with no labour protection

- Lack of participation in management matters and poor participation in trade union activities

There is likewise concern expressed by many women's groups that the government's ratification of the World Trade Organization agreement will impact on women's economic situation even more negatively as did the structural adjustment policies which the country adhered to under the World Bank. Lack of opportunities has led hundreds and thousands of Filipinas to seek work as domestic helpers and entertainers abroad. Women overseas contract workers constitute 71 per cent of the total 132, 561 overseas contract workers (OCWs) who went abroad in 1992. Many of the complaints of the women OCWs have to do with maltreatment, non-payment of salaries and other contract violations as well as sexual abuse.

4. Reproductive rights

Reproductive rights, under the legal system of the Philippines, is not considered a right. However, the Philippines supported the Cairo Conference on Population and Development and adheres to the principle that reproductive right is the basic human right of women and couples to decide freely and responsibly the number, spacing and timing of their children based on their own decision, without coercion, discrimination and violence. It is however not framed in the context of human rights but rather within the framework of population and family planning policies.

In 1990, there were 60 million Filipinos, 49.7 per cent of whom were women. Of these, 17 million women were of reproductive age (15-44) years. During the period 1980-1990, 45 per cent of women were suffering from iron deficiency anemia. Many of the problems of malnutrition and maternal mortality and morbidity can be attributed to women's poor access to health services because of their unequal rights and status in society. Low gender consciousness among policy makers and thus under-investment in women's health as well as religious and traditional beliefs and practices justifying the bearing of too many children also affect women's health.

Existing legislation on reproductive rights show a bias on strengthening maternity and penalizing those who resort to abortion. The 1987 Constitution enshrines the rights of the mother and of the unborn child. Articles 256-259 of the Revised Penal Code penalizes any person who shall cause or practise intentional or unintentional abortion. There are bills filed in the Senate and Lower House that seek to impose even more stringent punishment for those who resort to abortion. A Senate Resolution calling for the investigation of the detrimental effects on the health of women of the Artificial Contraceptive Programme seeks eventually to ban their use. On the other hand, there are some bills which promote motherhood such as Republic Act 7900 providing incentives to all government and health institutions with rooming in and breastfeeding practices. Republic Act 7322, increases maternity leave benefits in favour of women in the private sector. The bias for motherhood and the extension of social and health benefits for reproductive purposes only to married women, leaves out many women who may bear children without the benefit of marriage. The criminalization of abortion also highlights the extreme pressure put on women who might opt to abort as a last resort due to poverty and other emergency cases such as illness of the mother or as a result of rape and incest.

D. Violence against women – a human rights issue

Violence against women is now recognized as human rights violation. For many years, this issue has remained invisible due mainly to the silence and the silencing of women in many societies. This has fortunately been changed by the vigorous efforts of women's groups and the commitment of governments to address this sensitive issue.

Violence against women refers to all forms of violence inflicted on women on account of gender whether this be in the public or private spheres. These forms include, but may not necessarily be limited to domestic violence, rape and marital rape, incest, sexual harassment, abuse of migrant women workers, prostitution and sex trafficking, abuse of women detainees and of women in conflict situations and such practices like clitoridectomy or policies of forced sterilizations or forced abortions. It includes a range of actions, behaviours that may be physical, phychological, emotional, verbal or sexual abuse.

1. Domestic violence

Domestic violence is deemed to be society's hidden crime. As there was no name for it in the past, incidents of this nature were reported as simply "physical injuries," "parricide" and the like which did not accurately indicate its real magnitude and gives the mistaken notion that it does not occur in society at all. A 1995 UNICEF study of 1,000 cases of domestic violence reported to the Department of Social Welfare and Development, the National Bureau of Investigation and the Philippine General Hospital, crisis centres and shelters, revealed the following findings:

- The two most prevalent forms of family violence are wife beating and sexual abuse of young women

- One act of violence leads to another form of abuse (e.g. verbal assault)

- Poverty and strained family relations contribute to the likelihood of abuse

- Four out of 10 victims do not immediately report to the authorities

- The trauma of abuse remains long after the commission of abuse

- Most incidences of domestic violence take place at home while the victim is alone. More than half of the incidents also occur at night

- Abusers under the influence of drugs as well as liquor as well as absentee parents make for a precarious situation for violence to occur

Laws that apply to domestic violence cases are found in the Revised Penal Code and the Family Code. Articles 263-265 pertain to grave physical injuries under which battering is often categorized. In the Family Code, wife battering is a ground for annulment of marriage and legal separation (Articles 36 and 55, Family Code).

While the issue of domestic violence is no longer hidden as it used to be many other issues remain:

- There is as yet no comprehensive family violence law that can tackle this issue thoroughly

- More training has to be conducted for the police and the justice system to be prepared for these cases

- More support facilities and services should be provided. Those that are existing are NGO initiatives. Haven, a drop-in-crisis centre run by the Department of Social Welfare and Development and the Congressional Spouses Foundation is a step in the right direction

- More public education about the issue and the gender sensitivity training of men in general is urgently needed

2. Rape and sexual abuse

According to the Philippine National Police (PNP), women as old as 80 as well as babies aged eight months old have been raped. The agency reveals that rape occurs at one every six hours and only two out of 10 rape incidents are reported raped. From 1991 to 1993, there was an increase of 25 per cent (1,828 to 2,285 cases) according to the PNP statistics. Rape cases in general reveal the followings:

1) Most of the victims are young women with children below 18 years of age comprising more than half with a mean average age of 16;

2) Most of the victims come from lower classes;

3) Offenders are much older than the victims with an average mean age of 30;

4) A majority of the rape incidents involve people who know each other while stranger rape constitutes a small percentage of cases;

5) The majority of the offenders use a weapon or other device of coercion such as a gun, knife, or rope;

6) The closer the relation of the victim is to the offender, the more likely it is that the incident will not be reported or reporting will be delayed.

In recent years, the country has seen more heinous crimes committed against women involving not only rape and gang rapes but the murder of the victims. New information technology such as the Internet and the proliferation of pornographic videos and films have likewise contributed to the general climate of violence against women.

An Anti-Rape Bill is now in its Second Reading in the Congress of the Philippines that will reclassify rape as a crime against persons not as a crime against chastity and make more stringent the penalties for rape. Despite these efforts, rape incidents are alarmingly high and the following issues have to be tackled:

- More gender sensitivity training for agencies and law enforcement people so as to minimize the trauma of victims reporting to them

- Stricter enforcement of the law and public education warning of the dire consequences of the crime of rape

- Review and assessment of the impact of the media (e.g. advertisements and movies) as contributory to the culture of rape

- Assertiveness trainings to girls and young women in dealing with the threat of rape

- Passage of the Anti-Rape Bill

3. Sexual harassment

With the recent passage of the Anti-Sexual Harassment Law, there are now more women willing to testify in cases of sexual harassment and even rape. A study of the Samonte University Campus in 1992 involving 281 respondents (including students and faculty members) had the following findings:

- Most of the victims (87.2 per cent) were not aware of any university policy on sexual harassment

- Of the 71 students who admitted having been sexually harassed, 54 did not report the incident

- A greater percentage of faculty members experienced sexual harassment compared to students

- Victims did not report due to fear, embarrassment, avoidance of scandal and lack of knowledge as to what to do

It is in the workplace that many sexual harassment cases occur although a full scale study has yet to be done on this. In 1994, the Civil Service Commission issued a policy on sexual harassment in the workplace and the University of the Philippines drafted its own university policy at about the same time. Some issues need to be addressed urgently:

- Sexual harassment cases need to be better documented and publicized to embarrass perpetrators rather than the victims

- Establishments, schools and institutions have to evolve their own grievance mechanisms to deal with sexual harassment cases

- Education of men on the rights and fundamental freedoms of women

- Assertiveness training for women and young girls on how to detect sexual harassment

4. Prostitution and sex trafficking of women and girls

One of the most important issues in the human rights of women is the issue of prostitution. This issue is however clouded by the fact that most governments and societies while officially condemning it, are in fact tolerating it in their midst. The other factor that clouds the issue is the false dichotomies that have characterized the discussion of prostitution such as the distinctions of child and adult prostitution, the prostitution by choice versus the prostitution by force or forced prostitution and prostitution in the First World versus prostitution in the Third World. These distinctions make one practice acceptable and the other unacceptable (forced, child, Third World) but these distinctions have the effect of blurring the harm done to women and girls and makes prostitution seem compatible with women's quest for empowerment and dignity. From the perspective of human rights, prostitution is not really a choice; it is a false choice because one cannot choose to harm and denigrate oneself. The right that can be invoked here is not the right to prostitute or choose prostitution but the right not to be prostituted which is consistent with universal norms of human rights.

In the Philippines, a project group on prostitution examined prostitution as an industry that is composed of the bought (women and girls), the buyer (usually male clients) and the business (pimps, operators, agencies, brothel owners). According to this group, prostitution is still pervasive in the Philippines. The former bars and entertainment joints in Angeles and Subic Bay where the bases of the United States of America used to be located have now been taken over by the Australians, Chinese and the Japanese. Resorts and tourist areas like Boracay, Puerto Galera, Puerto Princesa, Cebu and other major cities have also been the areas where foreign tourists and local people flock for prostitution purposes. Apart from tourist areas, prostitution uses several channels like beer houses, karaoke clubs, expensive health clubs and sauna massage parlors. There is evidence of prevalent brothel prostitution everywhere but estimates are hard to come by.

Local trafficking for prostitution purposes does occur but this is less visible compared to sex trafficking internationally. The export of entertainers to work in Japan is a policy that can be construed as disguised trafficking as agencies which reportedly recruit young women for legitimate "entertainment" purposes, in fact put women in precarious situations leading to prostitution. In Japan alone, reports indicate that there are 100,000 women entertainers, a large percentage of whom are illegal workers. Cases of trafficking have been documented in Europe, in Malaysia via Sabah and Palawan, in Taiwan, Province of China and Hong Kong, China and also in the Unites States of America. Migration for work by large numbers of women have become easy channels for trafficking and thousands are victimized through this route.

In recent years, there have been a significant increase in the number of Filipinas marrying foreigners via mail order system, marriage introduction systems, Pen Pal Clubs and even via satellite as in the case of the Moonies. Marriage matching has become a lucrative business victimizing thousands of women along the way.

The response on this issue has been to introduce legislation to ban the matching of Filipino women for marriage to nationals on a mail order basis and other similar practices. This practice however continues because the same legislation does not apply in any other country where match making is legal. On the other hand, there are more decisive measures being evolved by countries to deal with trafficking of women and girls. One such measure in the Philippines is the filing of House Bill 6789 or the Anti-Trafficking of Women Bill. It identifies the various forms of trafficking and puts stricter penalties on offenders and mandates an Inter-Agency Task Force of the Government to implement measures and monitor cases. Similar Anti-Trafficking laws were passed in Belgium and in Australia but the latter dealt mostly with paedophilia.

Most of the research and assistance programmes have been innovations of NGOs which raised the issue as early as in the 1970s. The government is just beginning to catch up. More needs to be done in the following areas:

- Public awareness campaigns on the dangers of going abroad due to the possibility of victimization of traffickers

- More stringent screening criteria for prospective foreign nationals marrying Filipinas

- Review and assessment of tourist policies and regulations to abet sex tourism in the country

- Adoption of an Anti-Trafficking Law

- Empowerment and livelihood assistance and support services for prostituted women and victims of trafficking

- Human rights education and gender sensitivity trainings for law enforcement agencies dealing with victims of prostitution and trafficking

- More bilateral and multilateral agreements to deal with international trafficking syndicates and networks invoking the right to extraterritoriality

5. Women in armed conflict situations

Human rights violations in war zones is a continuing problem according to the Commission on Human Rights (1995). Women leaders, peasant women, militant workers and students suspected of subversion are harassed, detained and illegally arrested. Some of these cases end up in rape, torture and murder. Likewise mothers, wives and their children left at home were often caught in the crossfire and were targets of reprisals. From 1986 to 1993, 70 cases of human rights violations against women were reported. Half of these were murder cases and the rest were homicide, rape, extortion, illegal raid and seizure, ambush, robbery, disappearance, detention and indiscriminate firing.

Indigenous women are particularly vulnerable to the impact of militarization and armed conflict. Their struggle against big development projects which threaten their indigenous lands and ways, have sometimes been met with violence. Hardest hit are the indigenous women who are sexually abused, or are victimized in salvaging, hamletting, forced relocation by death threats, bombing of houses and farms, strafing, food and medicine blockades, rape and torture.

E. Challenges and opportunities in the promotion of women's human rights

The women's movement in the Philippines has achieved many gains in recent decades. Among them is the increased awareness of the rights of women and the government's stronger commitment to uplift the conditions of women. Alongside this is the growth of a vibrant women NGO community which at times is supportive and/or critical of government initiatives. Nevertheless, the existence of independent women's groups and a diversity of persuasions and political orientation make for a dynamic women's movement, all working for women's empowerment.

The task therefore of promoting human rights cannot be the work only of the Government, neither only of the NGOs. The government has made strong commitments in Beijing and Vienna to implement all of the human rights instruments it had ratified, foremost of which is the CEDAW. As a country with a very high level of awareness and sensitivity to human rights abuses due to the long years of repression under former President Ferdinand Marcos, the Philippines has led in human rights advocacy in the following: the creation of the National Commission on Human Rights, the inclusion of human rights in the educational curriculum and the writing of a Human Rights Plan for the Philippines.

Women's human rights has just been acknowledged recently but already, the Philippines has enthusiastically committed itself to its active promotion. The main impetus for this is really the existence of numerous, diverse and active women's groups that have taken on the task of monitoring specific forms of violations of women's rights. There are women NGOs that are concerned with legal advocacy (SIBOL, Women's Legal Bureau and Congressional Legislative Development), wife battering and family violence (Women's Crisis Center, LihokPilipina, Kalakasan), trafficking in women (Coalition Against Trafficking in Women Asia Pacific), violence against women (KALAYAAN), prostitution and trafficking (WEDPRO), migrant women (Network Opposed to Violence Against Migrant Women – NOVA) and many more. These groups are not just documenting cases and helping women but they are also, through their work, building the awareness and the jurisprudence for the laws and the policies of government to expand their understanding of human rights to include women's human rights.

The task towards full empowerment and gender equality as well as the elimination of discrimination will take generations to accomplish but the first decisive steps have already been taken and there is no turning back for the women of the Philippines.

VIII. UZBEKISTAN

CUSTOMS AND FAMILY LAW:
WOMEN'S RIGHTS IN UZBEKISTAN*

A. Introduction

The post-Soviet period set the scene for major political and economic changes in Central Asia with the rise of five independent states with Muslim majorities and a drastic revision of previous ideologies. The revival of indigenous cultural values represented by Islam has become one of the political catchwords of the newly independent states. As a result, the equality between men and women which was strongly associated with Soviet ideology (although such equality, nominally enshrined in the Constitution, was an ideal rather than a reality under Soviet totalitarian rule) became the target of strong criticism with the activation of religious and national consciousness. A clear trend towards a change in the social system emerged during the transition period. Despite the fact that the principle of equality continues to feature in the constitutions of the Central Asian republics, state authorities support a new patriarchal order based on the traditional role of women as mothers. In 1992 many official publications argued against the principles of equality denouncing it as an empty Soviet slogan.

This created a new space for the strengthening of social customs being adopted in family life, encouraging illegal polygamy and early marriages. These contradictions reflect a paradoxical reality in the Commonwealth of Independent States. On the one hand, women welcome the economic reforms and the new opportunities presented, including the establishment of free women's organizations but on the other hand there is a threat that women may lose their equality and their social rights granted under socialism. The transitional period has seen other contradictions arise too. There are high levels of education among women; yet there is a great passivity among women to adapt to the new social and economic realities. In the Soviet period, women were the object of the protectionist policy of the State. Now they themselves can influence the formation of policy on women through vehicles as the free women's organizations. But they have no experience. The mentality of the former Soviet citizens is slow to change.

These contradictions are a result of the double standard in the status of women during the Soviet period. Women enjoyed a number of political rights but these were not guaranteed in economic terms. Women were encouraged to be emancipated by the national legislation but at the same time, they faced restrictions on account of some traditional norms of behaviour in public and private spheres. Uzbek women are different from women in the West

---

* By Marfua Tokhtakhodzhaev, Women's Resource Centre, Uzbekistan.

in their views towards the state and their duties within their own communities, in which the male viewpoint of placing women in the family role predominates. The latter situation claims the subordination and submission of women to men and elderly members of the family. Uzbek women were and are conformists. Hence, there is a combination of two behavioural standards: the standard of modern women who must work outside of their home and who are professionals and educated, and the traditional standard, women who accept or submit to male domination. This has resulted in a collision in the behaviour of women and women are confronted with a dilemma: having to choose between the traditional and the modern way of life. The Soviet ideology pushed a woman towards modern standards; however, patriarchal family values pulled her back to play a traditional role of a daughter and wife. In post-Soviet times, a reversal to Muslim values, first and foremost, has greatly affected women. Modesty and subordination have become the major demand in the behaviour of women. Women are now "invisible" in the street and in public places, a requirement that Uzbek women demonstrate their identity as Muslim women by wearing veils. This new image is in stark contrast to the westernized image of most urban women that predominated in the Soviet time and now.

This situation shows that there was a hidden resistance to modern standards in the behaviour of the women not only in rural areas but in cities too. A sociological study conducted in 1993 showed that 55 per cent of young respondents preferred the traditional style of family life based on patriarchal values.

Marriage is considered a major cornerstone in an Uzbek woman's life; an unmarried woman is miserable and disdained by both men and women. So, to be married holds great value and is a goal of Uzbek women. Divorce is disfavoured. With all the above-mentioned problems, discussions regarding the new family law have lasted for more than one year, since the new law seeks to preserve all the main principles of equality of women in the family, inherited from the Soviet legislation on marriage and the family.

B. Legislation and the cultural context

Before independence in 1991, the Soviet Family Code entitled "The Fundamentals of Family Legislation, the Code of Marriage and the Family of the Uzbek Soviet Socialist Republic" was applied. This legislation remains in use today. In 1993 a new family law was proposed, based on equality between men and women in their family relations. This draft law was discussed for a few months and will now be complemented with new sections, which will reflect the cultural context. A comparison of these provides a glimpse of woman's legal status in Uzbekistan.

Before the October Revolution two laws operated in colonial Central Asia: Russian codes which regulated relations in society and which were common to all citizens, and Sharia laws which regulated relations within Muslim families and the Muslim sector of society. The first Soviet Constitution declared the political equality of women. The Decree on the Separation of the Church from the State, which abolished the Sharia courts, was met by militant resistance from the Sharia courts. Consequently, Muslim education and judicial systems continued in parallel with the Soviet systems of education and justice from 1927.

The abolition of the Sharia courts by the state did not, however, overturn the Muslim way of life as many norms in the domestic sphere were preserved informally and existed as national traditions in the consciousness of people who adhere to Islam. Throughout the Soviet period, contradictions between official legislation concerning the family and informal norms were conserved in the family relationship structure, between the different members within the nuclear family, husbands and wives, parents and children, men and women. Conflict within these relationships resulted in the inequality of women in the family.

Today, Uzbekistan is a secular state, although the majority of its population considers itself Muslim with the cultural context and lifestyle governed largely by Islamic norms. Amongst these cultural norms is the subordinated status of women in the family. Men expect women to be submissive daughters, patient wives and then respectful mothers of adult sons. Men dream about the continuation of these same roles of women in the present context. Modern men discuss amongst themselves the new legislation on family law and perhaps these prevailing attitudes will be a feature that will cause the decline of women's status in the future.

Currently, the Family Code of the Soviet era, based on the principle of equality of men and women in family relations (specifically in regard to personal and property rights) is implemented. The Family Code stipulates mutual spousal rights and obligations. All marital property acquired by the spouses during the course of marriage belongs to both parties in equal shares and is, upon divorce, to be divided into equal shares. Judges, however, have the judicial prerogative to derogate from this principle where it is considered judicially appropriate to do so. This provision in the code is often mis-used to subordinate the status of women in the family. For example, when a husband leaves his wife and children, the wife must wait for her husband's return, (often staying with her own parents) and fails to use the property acquired during the marriage. As the wife does not wish to be the initiator of divorce, the marital property is used by the parents or relatives of the husband or by the husband himself and the wife may find that she has, de facto, lost her share of the matrimonial property.

Divorce in the former USSR times was not difficult, especially if the application was made with the mutual consent of both spouses. However, at the same time, there were some legal provisions which aimed to protect women in these situations. For example, a husband could not divorce his wife if she was pregnant or if they had a child under one year of age. This provision has not changed. The rate of divorce in Uzbekistan is half that in the Russian Federation because of the strong influence of traditional social norms regarding women which requires them to remain submissive and not to create the circumstances which could lead to divorce. As a result, many women who may have valid grounds for divorce do not exercise their legal right to divorce for fear that their parents and relatives would hold them responsible for the breakdown of the marriage. Instead, they tolerate domestic violence, polygamy and humiliation for the sake of preserving the family unit and for the sake of their children. Women are aware that the threat of divorce puts them at a serious economic disadvantage.

Today, the main issues in divorce law concern the division and/or the maintenance of the matrimonial property. As noted earlier, current family law stipulates that property should be divided equally between spouses. This raises questions regarding the ownership of the family home. Will the home belong to both spouses as individuals each with a joint and full interest in the living space or will it belong to the family? This issue currently remains unresolved. Further, most women going through a divorce remain wholly unaware of the potential ramifications of the new property legislation.

Divorced mothers are entitled to child support from their former spouses but awards are notoriously low and inadequate. Whereas the legal mechanisms do exist to exact back payment from delinquent fathers, women are largely unaware of these and in many cases, are not inclined to seek legal counsel or utilize social services to ameliorate their situation.

The centrality of woman's role as mother is one aspect in the women's policy adopted by the Government of Uzbekistan. It believes that motherhood should command the nation's respect and esteem, and that it should be protected and encouraged by the state. And yet, in the promotion and protection of motherhood the fertility rate in the country is 4.3 per cent and the abortion rate is 50.8 per cent, with most of the population living in rural areas.

Abortion is legal and is the primary form of contraception. In 1989 the government eased the abortion law, expanding the period (from the twelfth to the twenty-eighth week of gestation) in which a doctor can legally perform an abortion. Family planning was a topic of debate in Uzbekistan in 1989 and has been negatively viewed by Uzbek writers and intellectuals who are of rural origin. On the other hand, the government supports the programme.

The proclamation of equal relations in marriage and the priority accorded to motherhood assigns to women special obligations. The fundamental concept underlying this point of view is the notion that the family is the building block of the state which serves to relegate women to the domestic sphere and their domestic responsibilities. Failure to comply implies not only disservice to the family but also to the state as well.

There was heated discussion on a proposal for a mandatory limitation of the work week to 35 hours for women with children under the age of 14 years. Many women writers, who had good wages and income, supported this. Such a protective viewpoint is tantamount to sacrificing women workers as unemployment escalates and the economy deteriorates.

It is especially important to analyse the co-existence of customs and traditions (often termed "Muslim") in private life and in the family. Soviet propaganda fought against the prejudices of the past, but this struggle was not successful because people had no desire for the state to interfere in their private lives and in the family. Therefore, many customs and traditions (both positive and negative) were preserved and many of them were diametrically opposed to the official legislation that existed.

Many customs and traditions are derived from Sharia laws and from folk customs rooted in the pre-Islamic religions of Central Asia which co-existed with Islam. Their existence sometimes seems strange in modern society. A few seem part of a medieval way of life that was not open and free. Many old customs and traditions were sanctified in people's consciousness as a part of their culture. It is for this reason that they remain and are not viewed critically. Customs related to marriage are an example.

Women usually do not have the right to marry on their own. According to tradition, they have to be given in marriage by a man. It is stated that the aim of marriage is reproduction, and therefore a woman who does not have a child can be divorced and her family must take her back. In rural areas, the norm is that parents decide the marriage match with the main deciding authority being with the father. In big cities and among the highly educated families, girls are given a limited say. Fathers who have common interests often decide on a match between their children in order to strengthen their linkages. Subsequently, when the interests of the parents go in separate directions, this often becomes a reason for divorce. Before the marriage, the parents of the bridegroom give "kalim" (a form of dowry), often a big sum of money and presents. Usually, a couple will go through a double wedding: a legally recognized civil marriage at the Town Hall and a ceremony at the mosque where their "nikak" (Muslim marriage contract) is orally sanctified.

One very detrimental social custom is that of holding lavish weddings. Weddings in rural areas are a holiday for the entire village population, entailing substantial expenditure. All family members work hard to be able to pay for the future weddings of the children. Even the elite of the nomenclature try to hold weddings according to this social tradition, though they do not display "kalim" and presents.

Polygamy existed during the Soviet period, especially in rural areas. It was not common in the cities. Now the idea of officially permitting polygamy has grown in favour, especially among the new rich who hold the view that if Islam permits polygamy, then it should be legalized.

Among the former nomadic population there exists a custom of bride kidnapping. Where some grooms cannot afford to pay "kalim" for a bride, they resort to bride kidnapping, often without the bride's agreement, with the bride's parents forced to give consent to the marriage in the name of the family honour.

The custom of adopting the children of close relatives also continues. A father can decide to give up his child for adoption to a close relative who has no child (or son). Alternatively, close relatives will often adopt those children who have lost their parents.

The idea of family privacy is not grounded in individual autonomy and integrity, but rather in the notion of the male right to control women and that it is women's duty to obey men. In addition, since law enforcement resources are overwhelmed by organized and violent crime, traditional cultural attitudes which justify women's subordination continue to prevail, with the result that cases of domestic violence are often ignored.

In conclusion, the social structure and social services are inadequate in addressing women's subordination in the family, including domestic violence against women in the family. Reproductive health services in the area of public health are often unavailable or, if available, then they are not accessible to all women. By reason of social custom, the number of well- educated women and professionals is on the decline which will only result in the further deterioration of their status. The revival of patriarchal values has its greatest impact in rural communities and among less educated women in the low urban strata of society.

IX. VIET NAM

PROMOTING WOMEN'S RIGHTS AS HUMAN RIGHTS*

A. Principles of equality

1. The Constitution

The 1946 Constitution of the Democratic Republic of Viet Nam for the first time established, on fundamental juridical grounds, the principle of equality between the sexes and immediately granted women the right to vote. Article 9 provides that "All power in the country belongs to the Vietnamese people, irrespective of race, sex, fortune, class, religion ..." and that "women are equal to men in all respects". With its implementation, millions of Vietnamese women citizens took part in power on an equal footing with men. Ten women were elected to the first National Assembly.

The 1980 Constitution gave more specific and comprehensive legal substance to the rights of women in all spheres: public and private, in all fields, political, cultural, economic, social and family (Article 63). In the area of employment, it directed the state labour policy to address the particular needs of women. Women enjoy equal pay with men for equal work. They enjoy pre-natal and post-natal leave with full pay, if they are state employees; they shall receive maternity allowances, if they are members of cooperatives. These constitutional provisions further directed the state to ensure facilities such as maternity clinics, kindergartens, canteens and other social welfare establishments to create favourable conditions for women to work, study and rest.

For the first time, the 1980 Constitution recognized the legal status of the Viet Nam Women's Union, with important attributions such as the right to submit draft laws to the National Assembly (Article 86). Therefore the Women's Union is striving to establish a close and permanent liaison with the women members of the National Assembly and people's councils of various levels with a view to promoting actions by the highest organ of state power in the drafting and passing of legislation and the supervision of law enforcement, in the areas related to women's life and labour and the protection of women and children.

With its constitutional mandate, the Viet Nam Women's Union has become the most active mass organization in the country, with a membership of 10 million. It organizes and mobilizes Vietnamese women of various strata, promotes their interests to help women secure equal rights with men in all fields. The constant awareness raising of women's role in productive labour and social activities to realize gender equality by the Viet Nam Women's Union is part of its significant contribution to the restoration and development of Viet Nam's post-war economy and culture.

---

* By Ngo Ba Thanh, Vice President, Viet Nam Lawyers Association, Viet Nam.

Thus, the government was among the first countries to have signed and ratified the Convention on the Elimination of All Forms of Discrimination against Women (CEDAW) in 1980. Immediately thereafter, it submitted the initial national report on its implementation in Viet Nam to the United Nations Committee on the Elimination of Discrimination against Women. These actions highlight the change in the legal status of Vietnamese women, in national as well as international law.

2. National instruments

The Constitution and the Penal Code are the legal instruments which support the government's policy to adopt appropriate legislative measures, including sanctions where appropriate, that prohibit all discrimination against women, in line with its commitment to CEDAW. The direct participation of 108 women deputies to the National Assembly makes possible the realization of women's aspirations into law. Of particular note, Article 125 of the new draft Penal Code sets out, in legally binding terms, internationally accepted principles and measures to achieve equal rights for women. It further sets out the available sanctions for anyone who resorts to violence or any other serious act to impede a woman's participation in political, economic, scientific, cultural and social activities. These sanctions range from a reprimand to a sentence of up to one year's re-education without detention or three months to one year of detention in more serious cases.

During 1984, the Communist Party of Viet Nam introduced directive 44 (1984) calling for an increase in the Viet Nam cadres contingent. In the same year, the Council of Ministers of the government adopted resolution 176a (1984) which calls for promoting women's role and capacities in socialist construction and national defence. Directive 44 highlights the urgent problems that need to be solved in the promotion of women's role in Vietnamese society. Whereas on the one hand the emancipation of women has seen women now making up the majority of the labour force (they are present in all branches, especially at the grassroots level), on the other, the vestiges of feudalist ideology need to be abolished along with the negative stereotypes about women to achieve full equality. Efforts to this end must be supplemented with concrete measures to effectively strengthen the contingent of women cadres in such areas as the assignment of women to key positions in leading organs of the party, economic and state managerial bodies, mass organizations, especially in those fields favourable to the development of their potential. Furthermore, efforts should be made to recruit more women members to the people's committees at different levels. Capable women should be appointed to managerial posts in agriculture and handicraft cooperatives and state-run economic establishments which employ many women. Women should be in the leadership of such establishments from central to grassroots levels and to those services largely related to women, such as public health, education, home trade, agriculture, light industry, finance, justice, social affairs and culture. Directive 44 also encourages women to promote themselves not only through their own endeavours and initiatives to overcome difficulties, but also to raise their standards and to increase their contribution to society.

Protection of women's rights is further strengthened by resolution 176a of the Council of Ministers. It specifies that at least one third of the People's Council (elected bodies) at all levels should be qualified women. Women must also be present in the people's committee (administrative bodies) at all levels. Moreover, it further urges that qualified women should also be eligible for promotion to key posts of the executive committees.

Resolution 176a also contains specific measures to strengthen the state's efficiency in enforcing women-related policies and to promote the role of the Viet Nam Women's Union. In the Office of the Council of Ministers and in all services and trades with a high proportion of women, or which are closely related to women's interests, specialists will be assigned to follow up and activate the implementation of policies and laws concerning women. The Viet Nam Women's Union has the right and the responsibility to submit to the state draft policies and laws aimed at ensuring women's full social participation and to join competent bodies in the monitoring and supervision of those relevant policies and laws. Once a year, the Standing Committee of the Council of Ministers and the Central Committee of the Women's Union will sit together to review implementation of policies and laws concerning women and to elaborate a new programme of women-related activities. Moreover, to enhance the consciousness of women's emancipation and equality between men and women, the political education of women remains an important task of the Women's Union.

More recently, resolution 04 (1993) and decree 37 (1994) reflect a state policy of recognizing the important role of women. They contain the objectives of improving the material and intellectual living conditions of women and of enhancing the social status and equal rights of women. The liberation of women is recognized as not only the responsibility of all administrative levels of government, but also of society as a whole. As regards implementation, decree 37 requires that all levels of government and the party should aim to have at least 20 per cent of their positions filled by women. All branches of the state apparatus area are also required to improve their gender awareness, develop plans for training and retraining women cadres, increase the number of women employees and formulate policies to develop women's skills.

B. Marriage and the family

1. 1960 legislation

Change in the traditional role of marriage and family life in Viet Nam is essential for the liberation of women both in society and in the family. It was in keeping with this strategic task and national policy that the first law on marriage and the family was promulgated on 13 January 1960. The state guarantees the full implementation of free and progressive marriage wherein monogamy, equality between spouses are ensured and women and children's rights are protected. Premature marriage, forced matrimony, physical abuse of the wife, divorce proceedings by the husband while the wife is pregnant or the infant is under 12 months are forbidden.

The progressive outlook of the law on marriage and family can be seen through the following provisions: (a) Art. 14: both husband and wife are free to choose their occupation, to engage in political, cultural and social activities; (b) Art. 23: children born out of wedlock enjoy the same rights and assume the same obligations as within a legal marriage; (c) Art. 29: in case of divorce, the allotment of property will be based on the labour contributed by each party, on the property at stake and on the specific situation of the family; labour in the home is considered as productive labour; and (d) Art. 19: sons and daughters enjoy equal rights and assume equal obligations within the family.

The marriage and family law of 1960 was adopted when Viet Nam was still partitioned. Following reunification, this law was extended throughout the whole country by decree 76/CP of 3 March 1977.

Implementation of the 1960 law generally was positive. Although some old-fashioned habits persisted, the spirit of the law was grasped by the masses. As a result, no man can now beat or abandon his wife or take a concubine without fear of public opinion and the law. Young men and women know how to appeal to the administrative authorities or to the courts to defend their rights to a free marriage. Women know how to defend their right to conjugal happiness and how to free themselves from feudal matrimonial bonds. Today, women are plaintiffs in 60 to 70 per cent of divorce cases.

During 1982 a nationwide survey on the implementation of the 1960 marriage and family law was initiated. The findings concluded that overall the people are more conscious of the principles of freedom of marriage and of monogamy than they were of the principle of equality between men and women in the family. The popular conception of man's superiority and therefore the marital and parental authority of the husband in the home, coupled with the resignation of woman's role by women themselves, sometimes have a nullifying effect on the implementation of the law, such as in the area of domestic violence in the home. Therefore, long-term advocacy and educational work are necessary to ensure a correct application of the law on marriage and the family.

2. 1986 legislation

The new national policy concerning marriage and family life is clearly enunciated in the new marriage and family law passed by the National Assembly on 29 December 1986. Article 1 stipulates that: "The State guarantees the implementation of the regime of voluntary, progressive and monogamous marriage in which husband and wife are equal with a view to nurturing a democratic, united, happy and lasting family. Marriage between Vietnamese citizens from different ethnic groups or religious groups, or between believers and non-believers shall be respected and protected."

For the first time, it is expressly mentioned in the law that: "Husband and wife shall have the obligation to implement family planning." This duty is in line with the fourth national population and family planning policy pursuant to resolution of the Fourth Plenum of the Central Committee of the Communist Party of Viet Nam, which restricts the number of children per couple to two. It sets the age of the mother and father at the birth of their first child to 22 and 24 years of age respectively in urban areas, and to 19 and 21 years in rural areas. It further states that spacing between children should be three to five years.

The marriage and family law sets the minimum age of marriage for men and women at 20 and 18 years respectively. Non-consensual marriage is held contrary to the law as are certain prohibitive acts such as polygamy; where the marriage partners are directly related by blood, (jus sanguinis), where the marriage partners are directly related in law (de jure) as in the case between adoptive parent or foster parent and adoptive child; or where one of the marriage partners is infirm, mentally ill or not in control of his or her actions or has venereal disease.

Socialist values are applied in the area of matrimonial property. The common property of a married couple is deemed to comprise all the property acquired by each of the marriage partners, including professional and other legitimate income gained by the couple during the course of marriage and the property bequeathed or given to the couple. Husband and wife shall have equal rights and duties with regard to their common property. This includes the purchase, sale, exchange, borrowing and other dealings involving property of considerable value, which require the general consent of both husband and wife (Article 15). When one spouse dies and there is a need to divide the common property, it shall be divided in accordance with the law on inheritance. Husband and wife shall have the mutual right to inherit each other's property (Article 17).

When one spouse or both seek to apply for a divorce, the People's Court first will seek reconciliation of the couple. Failing this, the Court on securing evidence that both parties are acting of their free will shall grant a divorce if it is found that the couple can no longer live together and the purpose of marriage cannot be achieved. Divorces are increasing, especially in urban areas. The divorce rate is 1.2 per cent in rural areas and 3.32 per cent in urban areas. The percentage of couples living separately is 1.3 per cent in rural areas and 1.77 per cent in urban areas. Article 41 provides that: "When the wife is pregnant the husband may sue for divorce only one year after the birth of the child." This provision shall not apply, however, in the case where it is the wife who makes the request for divorce.

The legislation provides for division of property in divorce cases in accordance with the following principles: (a) personal property shall be kept by the owner; (b) common property shall be divided into two parts, taking into account the situation of the property, the specific situation of the family and contributions by each party; and (c) where a couple is still living with the whole family and their own property cannot be determined, the husband or the wife shall receive part of the family property in proportion to his or her contribution to the preservation and enlargement of the common property and to the family livelihood. This 1986 legislation also recognizes that the work in the family is regarded as production work. Therefore the right of the wife and under-age children and production and professional interests are protected in the division of property and divorcees have rights and duties vis-à-vis their common children. In consigning care and custody of children in divorce cases, the children's interests in every respect, are to be taken into account. In principle, nursing infants are consigned to the care of their mothers. The non-custodial parent is required to contribute to the cost of child support and education. If he or she delays or evades the contributions, the People's Court may order a deduction from his or her income to meet the contributions; these contributions themselves may be reviewed as necessary.

3. The civil code

A new civil code was recently adopted in Viet Nam. As the 1986 law on marriage and the family remains in effect until it is amended, this code does not regulate all relations on marriage and family. However, some of the provisions in this code refer to civil relations, as follows:

- Article 35 establishes the right to marriage according to the following principles. First, marriage shall be based on the principle of monogamy. Second, both men and women have the right to marry freely, without fear of coercion or duress. Furthermore the freedom to marry between persons of different ethnicity, nationalities or religions and between religious and non-religious groups is respected;

- Article 36 establishes the right to equality between husband and wife. Husband and wife shall have the same rights and obligations in all aspects of the family and in civil transactions. Together, they shall build a plentiful, durable and happy family;

- Article 38 establishes the right to divorce whereby wife or husband, or both together, shall have the right to request the court to terminate their marital relationship for a legitimate reason.

4. The penal code

(a) Violence against women

Even though the issue of gender-based violence is not specifically addressed in these legal instruments, the new trend in national and international legislation is under way to extend the general prohibition on gender-based discrimination to include gender-based violence.

Article 125 of the Penal Code features infringements on the equal rights of women to participate in political, economic, scientific, cultural or social activities. Infringements of these rights are subject to (a) a caution, (b) no custodial reform for a period of up to one year or, (c) a term of imprisonment between three months and one year. In addition, there are other penal sanctions to punish infringements upon human life and dignity including rape (Article 112), forcible sexual intercourse (Article 113), sexual intercourse with a minor (under the age of 16 years) (Article 114) and the trafficking and trading of women (Article 115).

In the area of trafficking of women, measures by the state not only include legal sanctions, civil remedies and avenues for compensation, but also involve preventive measures such as public information and education programmes as well as protective measures such as support services for victims of violence. Documented instances of the violence against women covered by penal provisions are contained in the four tables in this section.

Table 1. Number of criminal cases tried for rape, trading and maltreatment of women, 1990-1992

	1990	1991	1992
Rape	293	214	332
Trading in women	81	133	161
Maltreatment of wives	23	27	35

Source: *Statistical Year Book*, Government Statistical Office of Viet Nam, 1993.

Table 2. Documented instances of trading in women, 1990, 1992, 1994

	1990	*1992*	*1994*
Viet Nam	40,000	80,000-100,000	130,000
Ho Chi Minh City	..	..	50,000

Source: *Crime in Viet Nam: Situation, Reason and Solution*, PPH, 1994.

Table 3. Percentage distribution of trade in women by economic status, January to March 1994

	Percentage
Unemployed (no job)	76.6
Government employee	7.0
Other economic status	16.4
	100.0

Source: *Crime in Viet Nam: Situation, Reason and Solution*, PPH, 1994.

Table 4: Percentage distribution of trade in women by educational attainment, January to March 1994

	Percentage
Illiterate	11.0
Primary education	35.0
Lower secondary education	28.0
Upper secondary education	26.0
	100.0

Source: *Crime in Viet Nam: Situation, Reason and Solution*, PPH, 1994.

(b) Bigamy or polygamy

Whereas the penal provisions for bigamy, whereby any married person marries or enters into a de facto relationship shall be subject either to a caution or non-custodial reform (for a period of up to one year) or to a term of imprisonment (for between three months and one year) (Article 144), feudal ideas still have an influence on women's role in the family. Hence, in practice, if a wife has no child, with his family's agreement the husband would unilaterally take another wife, leaving the former wife no option but to agree or to divorce. Conversely, if the husband is childless, his wife has no alternative but to endure. Thus, polygamy still exists in Viet Nam.

(c) Involuntary marriages

Article 143 concerns forcible marriage, i.e. forcing persons to contract a marriage against their will or preventing them from contracting or continuing a marriage (in which they have freely entered) by means of persecution, ill treatment, mental abuse, claiming of property or other methods. Legal sanctions range from a caution to a non-custodial reform (for a period of up to one year) or to imprisonment (for between three months and three years).

(d) Offences involving minors

Penal provisions concerning offences against minors include the contracting or entering into a marriage with a minor (Article 145), incest (Article 146) and the kidnapping, trading or fraudulent exchange of a child (Article 149).

To curb the above-mentioned offences against women, experience has shown that social development plans must deal with gender issues in a programme for socio-economic development, wherein the protection and development of women go hand in hand with the development of the country.

5. Nationality

Viet Nam grants women equal rights with men to acquire, change or retain their nationality. The Viet Nam legal system has discarded the theory of women's legal incapacity upon their marriage. Vietnamese women who marry a foreign national shall not be forced to adopt the nationality of her husband. The state also extends to women the same right as men regarding the nationality of their children. These provisions are in line with Article 9 of the Convention on the Elimination of All Forms of Discrimination against Women.

Article 1 (3) recognizes Vietnamese citizens as having only one nationality: Vietnamese. Marriage, divorce and annulment of unlawful marriage between a Vietnamese citizen and a foreigner will not change their respective nationality. Furthermore, if a husband or wife should either be granted or lose their Vietnamese nationality, there shall be no change to the nationality of the spouse.

C. Employment and labour rights

In Article 63 of the Constitution, it is stipulated that "Men and women shall receive equal pay for equal work". Article 7 of the Labour Code of 1994 provides that "Every one has the right to work, to freely select their occupation and trade, to undergo vocational trading and to improve their professional qualifications without discrimination with respect to sex, ethical and social origin or religious belief. The State therein prescribes regulations concerning the labour regime and social policies that are designed to protect women workers. These provisions are reinforced in the Civil Code. Article 45 of the Civil Code on the right to work stipulates that "Every person shall have the right to work, the freedom to choose a job or occupation without being discriminated against on the ground of his or her gender, ethnicity, social status, belief or religion".

Chapter 10 of the Labour Code contains specific regulations concerning women workers. Article 109 stipulates the state's guarantee to women the right to work in full equality with men in all fields. It is the state's policy to encourage employers to create the conditions that not only ensure women permanent employment but also provide them with access to a large spectrum of job opportunities with flexible working schedules, e.g. ranging from part-time jobs to jobs that may be done at home. The state also designs policies giving preferential treatment to women (i.e. affirmative action). The state grants tax reductions to enterprises employing a large number of women workers. Therefore, employers must recruit women workers on a priority basis if they meet the selection criteria for recruitment. To these ends, the state has designed policies and measures that gradually expand employment, improve working conditions, enhance professional qualifications and at the same time harmoniously combine working and family lives. Supplementary to the above, state agencies are responsible for organizing many types of training programmes for women workers to furnish them with occupational skills that are easily compatible with the physical and physiological characteristics of women and their roles as mothers.

Employers are strictly forbidden to discriminate against women or hurt either their honour or their human dignity. Employers must abide by the principle of equality between men and women in recruitment, promotion and remuneration. Employers are not allowed either to dismiss or unilaterally to end a labour contract of a woman worker for reasons of marriage, pregnancy, maternity leave or nurturing an infant who is less than 12 months old. Dismissal is permitted in such cases only if the enterprise itself ceases to operate. At the same time, the pregnant woman worker may herself unilaterally terminate her contract, without being required to pay any compensation, if her doctor certifies continued work would have harmful effects on the unborn child (Article 41, Labour Code). The interests of women workers during pregnancy are outlined in Articles 141-144 of the 1994 Labour Code. This guarantees that a woman worker, after delivery of her child, will retain her former position. Moreover, there are provisions which entitle women workers to social insurance allowances or allowances from employers that are tantamount to social insurance allowances, in such cases as taking temporary leave of absence for parental medical examinations, for implementation of family planning measures, or for the care of ill children under the age of seven years old. The Labour Code further obliges an employer of an enterprise engaging a large number of women to assist in the organization of creches and kindergartens or for financing part of the costs borne by mothers whose children are in creches and kindergartens.

Furthermore, Article 113 seeks to curb the employment of women workers in work considered dangerous or which involves contact with noxious substances, which may be harmful in respect of their childbirth and child nurturing functions. A list of these jobs is published by the Ministry of Labour, Invalids and Social Affairs. Additionally, any enterprise employing women workers in such work also must formulate a plan not only to provide professional training but also: (a) gradually transfer women workers to other appropriate jobs; (b) increase health protection measures; (c) improve working conditions; or (d) reduce the working time. Underground mining work or work that requires the immersion of the body in water are specifically prohibited.

Finally, Article 118 of the Labour Code stipulates that an enterprise employing a large number of women workers must assign a member of the senior management staff the task of dealing with issues relating to the rights and interests of women and children. In carrying out this task, employers must consult representatives of women workers. Membership of labour inspection teams must also include an appropriate proportion of women.

This progressive body of protective legislation for women workers is applicable to women employed in the formal sector. Although it is intended to enhance the well-being of women workers, there are increased costs to be borne by private employers. As a result, instead of protecting women, these provisions may become an impediment to women's equality in employment. These provisions in the Labour Code do not cover the vast number of women whose labour either in the home or in the fields goes unrecognized and their rights remain unprotected despite constitutional guarantees of the right to work for men and women. The Viet Nam Living Standards Measurement Survey (LSMS) 1992-1993 shows that 93.5 per cent of men and 91.8 per cent of women are economically active. The overall unemployment rate is 7.4 per cent. Women account for approximately 60 per cent of the unemployed. An estimated 30 to 35 per cent of the population is underemployed. In agriculture, where 67 per cent of the population are economically active, women assume about 60 per cent of the workload, in addition to their responsibilities in the home. Moreover, in the implementation of policies for the economic renovation of the country ("*Doi Moi*"), the household economy is being extended beyond the subsidiary economic activities, such as production of agricultural land, poultry and livestock breeding and growing vegetables.

With the policy of economic renovation, there is a new role for the household as the main unit of production. With its implementation, more traditional roles and values are being reasserted in the family household and the workload of women in both the field and at home is being intensified. However, it is too early to assess the impact of the new family household policy together with the new Land Law of 1993 on rural women. A national symposium on women and agriculture organized by the Food and Agriculture Organization of the United Nations and the Ministry of Food Industries (now the Ministry of Agriculture and Rural Development) concluded that while the rural household generally benefited from recent economic reform, women still have less access than men to farm technology, technical knowledge, savings and operating capital. Moreover, to ensure that widespread growth in productivity, new agricultural technologies and educational services have to become equally accessible to women farmers as well as men farmers. Acquiring this access may require the development of specific policies for women to ensure women and men can increase their agricultural productivity and at the same time increase their employment opportunities outside the agricultural sector.

D. Land rights

As a result of the 1992 Constitution, a new Land Law was passed on 14 July 1993 to implement specific constitutional provisions in the Land Law and national policies. Compared with the Land Law of 1988, new provisions in Article 2 provide that the tenure of the land use right is recognized as having juridical effect to provide to those who are using land on a stable basis the granting of certificates of land use rights by authorized state bodies. The Land Law provisions specify that the state shall protect the legal rights and interests of land users whereby any household and individual shall have the right to exchange, transfer, rent, inherit or mortgage the right to use land allocated by the state. The land is allocated for stable and long-term use.

According to a study made by the Centre for Family and Women Studies on the household economy and gender relationship, the de jure household head stands first in the list of household registration and he or she is the household representative in name as well as in official papers. De jure household heads in rural areas at present are mostly men who account for 73.1 per cent of rural households. Of the remaining 26.9 per cent, heads of household are either widows, single women bringing up their own children or women with migrant husbands working in the state sector. Whereas there may be no difference in the economic power or representational rights of male or female heads of household, in reality the latter usually have fewer labourers and less land. Furthermore, and possibly as a result, in the village their voice in meetings may carry less weight than those of male heads of households.

Under the Land Law, farming households have the right to exchange, transfer and rent as well as inherit and mortgage their right to land use. Since 1995, more than 5 million hectares of agricultural land have been allotted to more than 7 million farm households by certificates of land use rights. However, this allocation procedure affects women and men differently, with negative impact on women in the following areas: (a) titling of the land use certificate; (b) laws and rights regarding inheritance; (c) control over irrigation and other infrastructure; and (d) access to secondary benefits such as credit and extension services.

The titling of land use rights certificates provides for only one name, usually the male head of the household. A woman, as the spouse of the head of the family, will inherit the land use right upon his death. A literal interpretation of this provision in the strictest sense could mean that a woman farmer can only inherit land use rights as a corollary of inheritance and that she has no right to exchange, transfer, lease or mortgage the land use rights. Further, not having the two spouses named on the deed may also affect women's rights to access to benefits such as credit and extension services.

E. Legal and civil matters

Viet Nam's first Civil Code was adopted by the National Assembly on 28 October 1995 and took legal effect on 1 July 1996. Women's equality with men before the law in areas of civil law where women have traditionally been discriminated against is given full recognition. The Civil Code affirms the constitutional guarantees of social equality and human civil rights for all citizens in the political, civic, economic, cultural and social fields to prescribe human rights standards for equality in all legal and civil matters.

In line with CEDAW, Vietnamese women under the Civil Code enjoy legal capacity identical to that of men and the same opportunities to exercise that capacity, with equal rights to conclude contracts and to administer property. The Civil Code further protects individual personal rights, i.e. rights personal to the individual which cannot be assigned or transferred except in limited situations provided by law. These rights include inter alia: (a) the right to one's name; (b) the right to identification of ethnicity; (c) rights to protection of life, health and honour; (d) the right to marriage; (e) the right to equality between husband and wife; (f) the right to divorce; (g) the right to citizenship.

F. Reproductive rights

Reproductive rights are founded upon principles of human dignity and equality. Women have a unique role to play in human reproduction and they are directly affected by government policies. Therefore, a reproductive rights perspective can enable us to identify numerous strategies for social and political change and to seek policies and laws that improve women's lives. It is important to note that there is an international basis for women's demands for reproductive self-determination. Widespread recognition of the legal foundation for such claims to self-determination is a first step towards ensuring that reproductive rights become a de facto right for women around the world.

Viet Nam has a high population growth rate. By April 1993 the population had reached 70,642,000, which is 3.5 times greater than in 1940. Viet Nam ranks thirteenth in population size and fifteenth in population density among 164 countries in the world. It has maintained an average rate of population increase of 2.2 per cent nationwide in the last 10 years. With its current population growth rate, Viet Nam will have a projected population of 80 million in the year 2000.

Whereas Viet Nam has been successful in achieving many of its social objectives, most notably in the areas of literacy, birth control and the shifting of attitudes towards small family norms, the reduction of mortality and improvements for the survival of both infants and children, there is a need to achieve the same successes in several other social objectives which have implications for population policy, namely, malnutrition, poverty, rural-urban living standards and gender inequalities. The emerging macroeconomic structures and the new microeconomic conditions resulting from the shift to a market economy within a socialist framework have exacerbated some of these problems. There appear to be growing income inequalities and problems in ensuring that as GNP per capita rapidly increases, social development objectives also continue to be as successfully achieved as they were in the past. There is also the possibility that gender inequalities may be increasing. With a user pays system for example, the increased costs of education for families often lead to choices which favour boys over girls in a family.

With economic renovation and the introduction of the new system of economic management in the rural countryside, the family household has become a self-managed economic unit, whereby children become an important source of manpower for the development of the household economy. The concrete consequence of having more children and thus, more members in a family in terms of the Land Law provisions entitle a family to receive more land allocation. Hence many children living in the rural and mountainous areas have dropped out of school at the ages of 11 or 12 years to help their parents. While an urban married couple desires just one or two children, rural farmers wish to have more than two. Besides being a source of labour, Vietnamese people believe an old Confucian precept that every child is a source of happiness bringing good fortune. However, husbands and their relatives often openly favour sons over daughters because they will preserve the family line. Such attitudes in an agricultural country with 80 per cent of the population living in rural and mountainous areas, such as Viet Nam has contributed to an increasing number of children in the family. Moreover, many wives have to fulfil their husband's wish by having sons. After three or four births without delivery of a son, wives can be maltreated, and in some cases even beaten by their husbands or their families. Moreover, men may commit adultery or get married illegally, a return to the feudal pattern of family life. This has meant that the goals of the Fourth National Population and Family Planning Programme, in particular the delayed age of couples to have children at 24 and 22 years for men and women respectively have not been achieved. In fact, early marriages in recent years resulting in teenage pregnancies have occurred in violation of the marriage and family law. In de facto marriages, young women become mothers quickly and fail to space births. The result is trouble, unhappiness, undesired childbirth, ill health and relationships often ending in divorce and women engaged in prostitution.

In many instances, undesired childbirth is caused by an inadequate understanding of contraception and the unavailability of contraceptive services. Not long ago, the family planning campaigns were carried out in such a way that people understood that it was only the women who were involved in childbirth. Many husbands did not use any contraceptives. Furthermore, they would also prevent their wives from so doing. Today, people understand that population and family planning can only be successful when they promote full awareness and responsibility among both husband and wife and ensure good quality service and various contraceptive methods together with information. Nevertheless, the education of the whole population and especially men about the importance of women's health and well being, as part of a productive labour force is needed.

The development strategies for the advancement of Vietnamese women to the year 2000 should see the state increase the budget allocation for health care and social services and develop health programmes for Vietnamese women in the following ways: (a) to enhance the health care movement for women and children through guidelines implemented by local authorities in coordination with mass and social organizations; (b) to implement actively a primary health care programme, expanded immunization and malnutrition prevention programme, with special priority being given to women and children; (c) to strengthen the information, education and communication activities on the prevention of sexually transmitted diseases, particularly HIV/AIDS; (d) to improve working conditions and reduce labour intensity for women so they can enjoy leisure time; (e) to enhance communication on population issues to the remote areas and to households and individuals, integrate education about the population into the general and technical schools making the programme responsive to the specific groups and to have a separate programme for girls and young women; and (f) to strengthen and improve family planning services, and networks to the grassroots and to provide and make widely available safe and convenient family planning services responsive to users' needs.

G. Women's rights as human rights

For the last four decades, the Vietnamese woman has step by step through a hard-fought struggle won her equality on the triple plains of race, class and sex. The emancipation of Vietnamese women has kept pace with the Revolution. Gradually, that equality has developed de facto to the rhythm of the development of society and this process in the living reality has been recognized de jure in the legislation of the state, at every historical stage.

Right from the start, the Vietnamese revolutionary state founded by President Ho Chi Minh introduced in its first 1946 Constitution the principle, which has become immutable since then, of equality between man and woman. Article 9 provides that: "All power in the country belongs to the Vietnamese people irrespective of race, sex, fortune, class, religion and that "women are equal to men in all respects". In view of the aforementioned histor background, the following facts cannot be separated. The Vietnamese woman won equ with man only because she participated in the social and political struggle and in prod work.

As underlined in Viet Nam's country report to the Beijing Conference, recently in process of renovation ("*Doi Moi*"), resolution 4 (1993) and decision 37 (1994) reflected the recognition by Viet Nam of the important role of women and made clear the state's present goals in the struggle for women's emancipation, to improve the material and intellectual living conditions of women; to enhance the social status and equal rights of women; to stress that the liberation of women is the responsibility of all administrative levels of government, the mass organizations, of every family and of the whole society and to underline the role of Vietnamese women in implementing socio-economic goals.

Historically, Viet Nam has had clear views and policies on the role of women which found expression in its system of laws and regulations as well as through the implementation of the adopted policies, to facilitate the participation of women in development activities. This forms a good basis on which to help Vietnamese women to make progress and to enhance their role and status in the cause of national development. Yet the aftermath of a long war and the backward state of a poor economy, as well as the high population growth rate, has left the health of many women in an alarming state in some rural areas. Seventy to 80 per cent of pregnant women suffer from anaemia and 42 per cent of children under the age of five years suffer from malnutrition. The consequences of war were heavy: 4 million invalids, 300,000 orphans and millions of old people without a source of support because their children had died in the war. The number of widows and single women is high at 1,420,000. Even now, many women still give birth to deformed babies due to the effect of toxic chemicals sprayed during the war. A symposium on the long-term effect of the massive utilization of defoliants and herbicides during the Viet Nam war on nature and man concluded inter alia, that the existence of dioxin in the Vietnamese population and environment destroying the eco-system is a type of warfare that exposes present and future generations. This is yet a further form of human rights violation against women in situations of armed conflict, with acts which constitute violations of fundamental principles of international human rights and humanitarian law.

Viet Nam's country report to the Beijing world conference, in its Objective 9 aims to ensure women's equal participation in preserving and strengthening peace in Viet Nam and to contribute to the maintenance of durable peace in the region and the world. Actions to this end include mobilizing women to voice their views and perspectives, to take part in the reconciliation efforts and in the settlement of conflicts and to discuss and take part in policy-making regarding security and national defence.